THE END OF POLITICS?

The End of Politics?

Explorations into Modern Antipolitics

Edited by

Andreas Schedler

Assistant Professor of Political Science
Institute for Advanced Studies, Vienna

First published in Great Britain 1997 by
MACMILLAN PRESS LTD
Houndmills, Basingstoke, Hampshire RG21 6XS and London
Companies and representatives throughout the world

A catalogue record for this book is available from the British Library.

ISBN 0–333–65944–9 hardcover
ISBN 0–333–67403–0 paperback

First published in the United States of America 1997 by
ST. MARTIN'S PRESS, INC.,
Scholarly and Reference Division,
175 Fifth Avenue, New York, N.Y. 10010

ISBN 0–312–16295–2

Library of Congress Cataloging-in-Publication Data
The end of politics? : explorations into modern antipolitics / edited
by Andreas Schedler.
p.   cm.
Includes bibliographical references and index.
ISBN 0–312–16295–2 (cloth)
1. Democracy.   2. Populism.   3. Post-communism.   4. Privatization.
I. Schedler, Andreas, 1964–   .
JC423.E55   1996
320—dc20   96–20515
                                                                 CIP

Selection, editorial matter and Chapter 1 © Andreas Schedler 1997
Chapters 2–8 © Macmillan Press Ltd 1997

This book is printed on paper suitable for recycling and made from fully managed and sustained forest sources.

10   9   8   7   6   5   4   3   2   1
06   05   04   03   02   01   00   99   98   97

Printed and bound in Great Britain by Antony Rowe Ltd, Chippenham, Wiltshire

Contents

Notes on the Contributors

Gwen Brown is Associate Professor of Speech Communication, Radford University, Radford, Virginia.

Charles H. Fairbanks, Jr is Research Professor of International Relations, Johns Hopkins School of Advanced International Studies, Washington DC, and Director of the Foreign Policy Institute's Program in Soviet and American National Security Policymaking.

Barry Hindess is Professor of Political Science, Research School of Social Sciences, Australian National University, Canberra.

Erwin A. Jaffe is Lecturer at the University of New Hampshire, Manchester.

Norbert Lechner is Research Professor at the Facultad Latinoamericana de Ciencias Sociales (FLACSO) in Mexico City.

Louis Pauly is Professor of International Relations, University of Toronto.

Andreas Schedler is Assistant Professor, Department of Political Science, the Austrian Institute for Advanced Studies, Vienna.

Gershon Weiler was Professor of Philosophy, Tel Aviv University.

1 Introduction: Antipolitics – Closing and Colonizing the Public Sphere

Andreas Schedler

We live in antipolitical times. Many symptoms point in this direction: the reemergence of right-wing populism in western Europe, the antistate rhetoric of the new Republican Right in the United States, the recurrent success of antipolitical establishment candidates in Latin America, the ethnic recoding of politics in the former Soviet Union and Yugoslavia, the widespread evidence of popular disenchantment with politics in old as well as new democracies, the tangible presence of antipolitical motives in media discourse, and the emigration of sovereignty out of politics and into societal systems of global scale. This multitude of dispersed indicators naturally falls together into a colourful mosaic of generalized antipolitics. 'We live in antipolitical times'. Indeed this phrase is marvellous – the ideal opening of any book on antipolitics. It formulates a bold hypothesis, proclaims a new era, irradiates the air of grand theory and suggests an extraordinary capacity on the part of the author to capture the signs of our time. Let us therefore read it cautiously, with reservation. Or better, let us reformulate it.

Antipolitical discourses are nothing new in Western political history but today, in the late twentieth century, they have gained renewed prominence. They now form an important, at times even hegemonic element of the ideological universe. And in all probability they have still not reached the peak of their global career. After the presumptive end of ideology, antipolitics may even evolve into a post-ideological core ideology. So, after all, we may indeed be heading towards 'an antipolitical age'.[1] But we cannot be sure. To begin with, we do not even quite know what antipolitics actually is.

This introductory chapter aims at constructing the notion of antipolitics in a broader, more systematic, explicit and

1

abstract way than previous authors, who employed the term in more or less casual manners.[2] To do so, we distinguish, metaphorically speaking, two forms of antipolitical thought – pretensions to dethrone and banish politics as opposed to pretensions to conquest and colonize politics. In the first case, politics becomes unemployed and the public sphere is virtually vacated and left uninhabited; in the second case, politics becomes alienated and the public sphere subjected to 'foreign' rule.

These conceptual prolegomena will set the stage for the subsequent analyses. Some of them reconstruct antipolitical traditions in Western political thought which continue to nurture contemporary antipolitics (Barry Hindess, Gershon Weiler and Erwin Jaffe). Others focus on antipolitical discourses and behaviour present-day actors engage in (Charles Fairbanks and Gwen Brown). And still others describe what we could call structural antipolitics, the erosion of politics by objective societal trends (as well as by the corresponding antipolitical interpretations), such as its loss of territory vis-à-vis the transnational economic system (Louis Pauly and Norbert Lechner).

All authors share a willingness to take antipolitical discourses seriously, to study them in their own right. In the field of political science it has become commonplace to affirm that we live in times of political crisis. The rhetoric of crisis abounds: crisis of governability, crisis of the nation state, crisis of democracy, crisis of representation, crisis of political parties, crisis of ideology, crisis of confidence and of course, crisis of politics. The temptation is great to view antipolitics as a mere response to these critical developments, as an ideological superstructure derived from contradictions which have arisen in the foundations of politics. In contrast the contributors that make up this volume do not treat antipolitical discourses as simple dependent variables caused by political failure and crisis. Instead they comprehend them as variables of their own logic and weight.

REMOVING POLITICS

It is quite evident that if we want to speak about antipolitics in other than loose and stylish ways we cannot remain silent on the subject of politics. Before we know what the negative notion of antipolitics can possibly mean we have to explain how we conceive of its positive mirror image. So, let us begin with a concise (functional) definition of politics. In our view politics embraces three things: the definition of societal problems and conflicts, the elaboration of binding decisions and the establishment of its own rules. Politics delineates the realm of common affairs. It manages these collective affairs in an authoritative way. And it determines the rules and metarules which govern these operations.

This concept of politics is functional insofar as it defines politics according to the societal tasks it is supposed to fulfil. It is formal insofar as it does not postulate any preestablished material content of politics, such as security or survival. It is ahistorical insofar as it applies to all forms of society, to early 'tribal' societies as well as to modern complex societies. And it is amoral insofar as it does allow for states of dysfunctionality; yet it does not equate politics with all the niceties we associate with liberal-democratic politics, such as freedom, equality, compromise or conciliation.

In this introductory chapter we will argue that politics as defined above presupposes the existence of a community whose members are aware of their mutual interdependence as well as of their internal differences, who are able to act in concert and who are willing to accept authoritative decisions. We will argue as well that ideologies which declare politics to be harmful or at least redundant and thus propose to throw it overboard, that such antipolitical ideologies usually reject one of these four basic premises of politics. Instead of collective problems they see a self-regulating order; instead of plurality they perceive uniformity; instead of contingency they state necessity; and instead of political power they proclaim individual liberty. We will briefly outline these four guiding distinctions.

Public Action versus Self-regulation

Most definitions of politics underline its responsibility for both delimiting and managing, in a purposeful way, the realm of public affairs. Niklas Luhmann is wrong. It is neither the hierarchical polarity of power (top versus bottom) nor the antagonistic structure of conflict (government versus opposition), but the binary opposition between the private and the public which represents the primary code of politics.[3] By sorting communicative acts according to their political (public) or non-political (private) quality, this scheme decides, so to speak, at first instance whether they belong to the political sphere or not.

Of course the concrete dividing lines between the public and the private are not preestablished external givens. Politics is a self-defining, self-constituting activity which delineates its spheres of competence on its own. In the political game, people also discuss and decide what may legitimately be discussed and decided by politics. As a consequence the boundaries which separate the public from the private are not fixed but shift over time. They are moving targets. Far from being uncontroversial, they are objects of continual struggle. And they are not always clear-cut but often look blurred and indeterminate.

Yet the distinction itself between public and private affairs enters the world the very moment politics emerges. Both are of the same origin and they evolve together. Even in stateless societies where politics presents itself as an intermittent, barely differentiated activity still embedded in social life, even there this act of classification, the authoritative statement about which activities, motives and conflicts count as collective (as opposed to individual) constitutes a central part of the political process.[4] It is only in two cases that the dividing line between the public and the private objectively disappears: in totalitarian societies and on Robinson Crusoe's island (before the advent of Friday). While in the former case everything is political, in the latter everything is personal.

Yet antipolitical ideologies may still postulate that certain groups of families or individuals, though living in physical proximity, do not face any need at all for collective action. These people, the argument runs, do not form a community of interdependent members. They live in complete autarky, and they neither come into conflict with their neighbours nor feel the expediency of engaging in common projects. Collective problems requiring joint action do not exist, nor do conflicts arise which could not be settled spontaneously by the involved parties themselves. I do not need anybody, people say, and nobody bothers me. In this world that ignores all public goods other than self-generated ones and all public evils other than self-healing ones, in this self-regulating world politics appears to be a useless enterprise, or worse, a harmful one. It offers solutions for problems that do not exist. Its main functions, the management of conflict and the coordination of action, have become orphans. Resented as an improper interference in private affairs, it turns into a strange object of generalized contempt.

Such antipolitical utopias which represent the public space as a barren and deserted land and thus depict the place of politics as being vacant, appear in different settings. Sometimes they borrow their metaphorical core from biology. This applies, for example, to the populist idea of an organic, prepolitical community menaced, contaminated and sub-verted by politics. And it applies as well to the system-theoretical concept of societal 'autopoiesis' (self-generation) modelled on the structure of the human brain.[5] Yet, in modern times, the idea of a self-regulating order has found its paradigmatic embodiment in the suggestive metaphor of the market, the invisible hand. Classic liberalism contains an antipolitical core.[6] We may discern its antipolitical punchline, for example, in the proposal to establish a market society, that is, a society integrated by decentralized networks of exchange. But antipolitical motives are tangible in other liberal proposals as well, for instance, in calls to put basic rights out of political disposition, to keep politics out of most spheres of social life and to reduce the state to its minimal expression. The concep-tion of society as a self-propelled and self-sustaining machine driven (and held together) by market competition has found its conclusive expression in the neoliberal conviction that politics *tout court* is nothing other than a parasitic, rent-seeking activity.[7]

Plurality versus Uniformity

Politics presupposes difference – different values, different in-terests and different priorities, different conceptions of common goods and evils, different measures of efficiency and different assessments of trade-offs, different strategic calcula-tions and different instrumental choices, different time preferences, different assumptions about the future and different degrees of risk aversion. *Et cetera.* Politics is called upon to recognize, protect and reconcile these differences, to diffuse them and at the same time to assure their coexistence. *E pluribus unum.*

In the same way that politics presupposes plurality, homogeneity precludes politics. Communities without conflict have no need for political action. Where conflictual diversity has given way to harmonious uniformity, politics has become redundant. Where people share preestablished world views, where everybody knows what to do (and what to want), it is pointless to go through the trouble of forming, aggregating and integrating political preferences. Where collective interests are unique, given and evident, political actors fall victim to structural unemployment. Even worse, they arouse suspicions of introducing artificial conflicts and divisions into an originally harmonious community.

In the real world, homogeneous societies do not exist. In the world of political thought, however, various ideologies have indeed bred antipolitical fantasies of consensual, conflict-free, reconciled communities. They have conceived society as a single, unified actor, as a pre-Freudian megasubject liberated from the burden of politics, acting 'as one man' pushed ahead by nonambiguous and nonconflicting volitions. Think, for example, of the people in populism, the nation in nationalism, the revolutionary class in Marxism or the herd of faithful sheep in religious fundamentalism. Incidentally it is well known that such antipolitical theories tend to bear unpleasant political consequences. They contain the temptation to suppress the differences they ignore, to manufacture with violent means the societal unity they assume.

Contingency versus Necessity

Politics is the denial of fate. It rests on the assumption that things could be different and that we can do something about them. In the realm of necessity, under the grip of hard constraints, politics atrophies. Whether we associate it with collective action, power or decision-making, politics always presupposes contingency – margins of freedom, the availability of choice, openness, control of the future, the presence of alternative options, minimum degrees of sovereignty. Politics after all is the art of the possible, not the science of the impossible.[8] This is even true for 'tribal' or 'segmentary' societies which perceive themselves as firmly embedded in tradition, nature and transcendence. Even they have a certain demand for collective decisions. Applying and adapting ancestral rules, reading and manipulating nature, soothing the gods and bargaining with them, represent exemplary instances of political decision making. Performed either by specialists or by the collective as a whole, they transform uncertainty and indeterminacy into patterns of understanding and courses of action.[9]

Yet since its very origins, politics has always had to assert itself against external constraints. Earlier it had to defend its nascent latitude against the irresistible force of nature, God's authoritative arbitrariness and the immutable rules of tradition. In modern times it has had to impose itself, above all, against the nearly overwhelming dynamic of the market economy.

Since the 'long' sixteenth century the capitalist world-system and the system of nation states have evolved together in close interdependence. The existing asymmetry between a single economy of global reach and a multiplicity of territorially bound political systems is nothing new. It has been a constitutive feature of the modern age from its very beginning.[10] Yet it seems that the tension between transnational markets and national politics has augmented considerably since the early 1970s. Today, after Keynesianism, it has become commonplace to ascertain that democratic politics, tied to its national territory, has hopelessly fallen behind the global expansion of capitalism, technology and culture. Apparently the capacity to act has migrated out of the political system into other societal subsystems, and both have entered an unprecedented state of disjunction.

The nation-state's loss of control and sovereignty has found expression in countless diagnoses which speak of progressive 'ungovernability'. As mentioned, many of them are cast in the dramatic language of crisis. In most cases this semantics of crisis denotes a concern for politics, the wish to come to its rescue, to rethink or even reinvent it.[11] In contrast with such propolitical ambitions to transform and revive politics, other authors welcome the new constraints politics is forced to recognize. They applaud the disempowerment of politics and celebrate its impending disappearance. And they readily extend the benediction of inevitability to these processes. This is true, for example, of neoliberal technocrats who impose harsh programs of market reform on their developing societies and who tend to perceive (and to justify) their policies as the mere passive execution of inexorable economic laws.[12]

Authority versus Anything Goes

In the same way that a political community, in order to exist, needs to be free from external constraints, at least to a minimal degree, it must be able to impose internal constraints on its members. Politics implies the making of binding decisions. It defines rules and sets restrictions – consensual rules and self-restrictions perhaps, but rules and restrictions nevertheless. It is impossible to speak of politics and remain silent on power or authority. Most concepts of politics accordingly take this aspect to be its essential, defining quality. This applies to 'the authoritative allocation of values' as well as 'the production of collectively binding decisions', to cite just two of the most prominent system-theoretical definitions of politics.[13]

Historically, the sources and resources of political power, the means politics sets in motion in order to get its decisions socially accepted, have varied. In 'tribal' societies, political decisions acquired their binding force through ritual or the invocation of transcendent sanctions and rewards. In modern societies, legal violence, administered by its monopoly holder, the state, has developed into the ultimate backing of political power. In this Weber was right: the state represents the institutional core of modern politics and violence its distinctive means (even if today the tortuous 'diabolic' grip of politics tends to be more tangible in international than in domestic – domesticated – relations).[14]

The conceptual privilege Weber grants to violence follows from his equation of power and coercion. His 'vertical' notion of power, however, contrasts with an alternative, consensual approach which defines power as the capacity for cooperative action based on 'horizontal' obligations. More than anybody else, it is Hannah Arendt who is associated with this 'positive' idea of power that substitutes mutual promise for threat and fear.[15]

As with all other component parts of politics, the claims society makes on the resources of its members are open to principled 'antipolitical' criticism. Antipolitical individualism celebrates unrestricted subjectivity, antipolitical tribalism unrestricted collectivity (on a subcommunal level). Both versions of anti-authoritarian revolt follow the same anarchical impulse: anything goes. Why abide by the rules of the game? I do what I want. Hobbes's 'natural' state of civil war describes the limitational horizon such antipolitical notions of freedom disclose. Life before politics (as well as after it), life in the prisoners' dilemma: 'solitary, poor, nasty, brutish, and short'.[16]

COLONIZING POLITICS

The family of antipolitical ideologies discussed above qualifies politics as a redundant (as well as pernicious) activity. All these discourses question the validity of politics' fundamental preconditions. They share the conviction that the core function politics fulfils – the management of public affairs – is good for nothing. In essence they all claim that problems of collective action do not exist. We have outlined four lines of thinking. First, politics is unnecessary because society does not exist; there are no public goods or evils politics could possibly take care of. Second, politics is unnecessary because individuals do not exist and neither do social subgroups. The community therefore ignores conflicts as well as problems of coordination. Third, politics is impossible because there is nothing it can do about the issues and cleavages we are facing; the course of history is set, and politics has no choice other than to wait and close its eyes. Fourth, politics is undesirable because society is not entitled to extract any resources from its members or to lay any restrictions on them.

All these antipolitical ideologies aim at abolishing politics, at getting rid of it, or at least they fight to roll it back, to cut it down, to reduce it to its minimal expression. We now turn our attention to another version of antipolitics, namely to efforts at 'colonizing' the political realm. This colonial variety of antipolitics concedes the functional value of politics but

denies that it ought to be conducted according to its own laws
and logic.

Politics and Language

In modern times politics has become an autonomous sphere
of action, a societal subsystem driven by its own logic and dynamics. Yet the evolution of modern politics, its societal dis-
embedding, differentiation and emancipation, has been
anything but a smooth process. Nor has it formed, once
achieved, a self-sustaining, self-reproducing equilibrium. The
external boundaries of politics have not been drawn by un-
wavering and unstoppable evolutionary processes but have
emerged as contingent outcomes of conflicts. Systemic boundaries are battlefields and the autonomy of politics is a fragile
creature. Unable even to pacify its historical front line against
religion, modern politics faces periodic threats of invasion
from numerous other societal subsystems which try to replace
it by its own operating principles. It has to defend its frontiers
against pretensions to import or to impose, for example, the
logic of money and markets, science and technology, entertainment and advertisement or family and intimacy.

This image of politics as colonized by non-political modes of
action leads to a tricky question. What is so special about politics? In other words, what difference is there between political
and non-political modes of communication? What distinguishes the political topography from the landscapes we find
in non-political territories? What difference does it make if
politics does or does not fall under 'colonial rule'?

Up to now, from a normative point of view, we have relied
on a 'lean' notion of politics. Of course our functional
definition of politics admits the possibility of dysfunctionality
or policy failure. Yet in contrast with approaches like Hannah
Arendt's that by definition place a high positive value on political action, we have avoided endowing politics with attributes
of moral goodness. Above all, we have been cautious not to
conflate politics *per se* with liberal democratic politics. Both
our concept of politics and its four fundamental premises are
fully compatible with illiberal and authoritarian forms of politics. Dictators do not deny the existence of public affairs (even
if they try to monopolize them) and they accept societal diver-

sity (even if they try to suppress it). They also hold political discretion in high esteem and, of course, the same can be said about the enforcement of political decisions. If we decided to recognize only liberal democratic politics as 'true' politics (as did Hannah Arendt, who equated politics with equality, freedom, and deliberation), we would be compelled to confer the title of 'antipolitics' on all non-democratic regimes and political styles. In our view, however, this would stretch the notion beyond its breaking point.

Therefore we will try to answer our question on the specific nature of politics by narrowing down our perspective to *democratic* politics. Thus our question now becomes: what is special about democratic politics? What distinguishes democratic forms of political action from non-political modes of communication? To find an answer we have to give up our moral abstinence in order to introduce stronger and more explicit normative assumptions. The assumption we would like to make is the following. In its everyday working liberal democratic politics relies on various media of communication, for instance on power, law or television. It cannot be reduced to just one of them. Its distinctive medium of communication, however, is language (or deliberation).

The point of distinguishing language as the primary medium of political decision making may be condensed into three main arguments. First, the ideal of open deliberation among free participants is based on the same constitutive principles as democracy: the principles of autonomy and equality.[17] Second, processing dissent through discussion holds the promise of rationality. Dialogue, as distinguished from monologic decision making, promises to reduce the probability of error. Third, language represents the classical opposite to violence, to external and internal state violence (war and repression) as well as to violence directed against the state (insurgency and terrorism). The word stands against the sword, the logic of arguments against the logic of power and war.

Basing politics on 'the forceless force' of the better argument (Habermas) is not exactly a brand-new proposal. Its genealogy goes back to Aristotle and includes both Hannah Arendt and Jürgen Habermas. Furthermore it has made a remarkable career in the last few years. A good number of authors have formulated similar projects of 'communicative', 'deliberative' or 'discursive' democracy.[18] Yet, in our view, the norm of deliberation potentially conflicts with competing norms of democratic representation. Above all it may violate the assumption that democratic elections, in order to be both meaningful and consequential, confer policy mandates to the winning parties. The consensual norm of deliberation may run counter to the majoritarian norm of electoral accountability.[19] Yet the growing attractiveness of the former may be due to the decreasing relevance of the latter. Perhaps the conflict between the two is empirically subsiding.

Today, in the late twentieth century the historical cleavages which laid the foundations for West European party systems[20] have lost their salience, and the party systems once inert and frozen have begun to thaw. In addition the fall of surreal socialism has deprived liberal democracies of their enemy, their systemic competitor, which adds to the new openness and fluidity of the situation. It is in this 'post-ideological', 'post-historical' or 'post-modern' context that a shift of emphasis from electoral mandates to deliberative policy making becomes both plausible and appealing. In this sense our claim that language represents democracy's distinguishing medium of coordination reveals itself as a relative, time-bound norm (which, however, does not diminish its validity).

Partial Rationalities

If we accept language and deliberation to be the hallmarks of democratic decision making, we can read antipolitical invasions of the political realm as efforts to subvert the communicative rationality of politics and to replace it with other, one-sided forms of rationality. Antipolitical colonizers try to reshape politics according to their own image, try to impose their own, partial rationality on it. We will illustrate this hypothesis relying on the Habermasian triangle of strategic–instrumental, normative and expressive rationality (which we will reformulate as a square).[21]

First, *instrumental antipolitics* aims at placing technocratic experts on the throne of politics. Treating the social world analogously to the natural world as a set of dependent variables, politics gets reduced to the calculus of adequate means.

Political resistance is seen to originate either from ignorance or from irrationality, and political discussion is dismissed as a waste of time which opens politics to corruption and inefficiency.[22]

Second, *amoral antipolitics* comprehends politics as a strategic power game, a marketplace where utility-maximizing participants endowed with fixed and exogenous preferences engage in quasicommercial exchanges of goods and favours. This standard rational-choice conception of politics clearly deserves to be qualified as antipolitical. It denies that any boundary exists between private and public action, and floods the political realm with private motives. If taken seriously the microeconomic approach to politics breeds simple and predictable results: political corruption veiled, embellished and justified through a language of rationality.

Third, *moral antipolitics* shuts down the arena of political debate by invoking material (as opposed to procedural) normative givens. Parting from fundamentalist convictions this variety of antipolitics strives to monopolize the definition and defense of goals it takes for immutable. It abhors dissent as amoral, opposes compromises as treason, disdains the pursuit of private happiness, rejects consequentialist ways of ethical reasoning and ignores the existence of moral dilemmas. Yet we should not overlook the fact that most moral codes contain certain antipolitical elements, that is, first principles which are set as absolute, unchangeable, inviolable, beyond the reach of political discussion. Think, for example, of the place equality and human rights occupy in liberal theory.

Fourth, *aesthetic antipolitics* subverts the power of words through the power of images. It downgrades political deliberation and decision making to mere acts of backstage performance and as a countermove pushes theatrical forms of action to the centre stage of politics. With aesthetic antipolitics the political sphere suffers from intrusion and foreign occupation by the logic of theatre and drama, rock and roll, sports and entertainment, design and advertising, the fine arts, television, religious confession, psychotherapy and intimacy. With aesthetic antipolitics the façade prevails over the face, beauty over truth, the symbolic act over verbal communication, the magic trick over the real measure, the virtual over the actual, the comforting ritual over the disturbing experience of learning,

character and the display of virtue over programs and the
evidence of success, the movie script over the speech manu-
script, the stuntman over the legislator, the symbols of family
life over the insignia of public life, the expressive codes of
short-distance relations over the moral codes of the public
sphere, the credible expression of emotions over the plausible
lining up of arguments, the excitement of the extraordinary
over the greyness of everyday life.

Our four varieties of colonial antipolitics represent mirror
images of Habermas's well-known colonization thesis. While
Habermas analyzed the political system colonizing the life-
world (jointly with the economic system)[23] we have been
talking about the life-world colonizing the political system.
Instead of looking at the imperialism of systemic mechanisms,
we have directed our attention to the imperialism of partial
rationalities generated in the life-world. In this sense the
forms of antipolitics we have analyzed may be regarded as
cases of 'inverted colonialism'.

EXPLORATIVE EXPEDITIONS

Let us recapitulate. We have sketched two families of antipolitics; or better, two tribes of antipolitics. One, denying that
politics can or should fulfil its function of societal coordination, aims at removing, replacing, abolishing, eliminating politics. The other one, undermining political deliberation in
favour of 'halved rationalities' (Habermas) imported from
other spheres of action, aims at colonizing, conquering, occupying, dominating, distorting politics. While the former would
be happy to lock up the public sphere and throw away the key,
the latter is more modest in its aspirations: it would be
satisfied to ease the deliberative burden which rests on the
shoulders of democratic politics.

The following explorative expeditions into antipolitics
address both ways of 'subverting' the public sphere. They
analyze pretensions of 'removing' politics as well as efforts at
'colonizing' politics. The borders are not always clear, and
sometimes both fields of antipolitics overlap. All in all,
however, the contributions follow clear priorities. Barry
Hindess, Gershon Weiler and Gwen Brown deal with actors

and discourses that threaten to invade politics. Erwin Jaffe, Charles Fairbanks, Louis Pauly and Norbert Lechner deal with processes and ideologies that threaten to remove politics. It would neither be honest nor credible to sell these analyses as a seamless whole, as a balanced and comprehensive, coherent and homogeneous piece of work. They resemble more a collage than a mosaic. Yet each chapter makes a distinctively original (and often surprising) contribution to the topic as a whole.

As we have outlined above, antipolitical colonialism provokes border conflicts. Any attempt to invade the political territory in order to impose 'foreign rule' cannot but put into question the established boundaries of the political. In his political–philosophical contribution Barry Hindess argues that such conflicts over the proper boundaries of the political are endemic to modern societies. The evolution of the modern state, this complex, remote and powerful set of institutions that monopolizes the elaboration of mandatory decisions, has given birth to a polar opposition, real as well as analytical, between state and society. As a consequence 'antipolitical' conflicts regularly arise along the borders between 'the state' and 'the society' (or 'the political community'). Both sides tend to perceive each other as contaminated fields of action and they either try to purify the other or protect their own innocence against perceived threats of invasion, contamination or corruption.

Language is the distinctive medium of democratic politics, we maintained above. Gershon Weiler's contribution can be read as a commentary on this quasi-Aristotelian (or Arendtian or Habermasian) assertion. Sharing this explicit 'logocentric' notion of politics, Weiler identifies Thomas Hobbes as a conscious opponent of Aristotle and as such, the father of modern antipolitics. In his perspective, Hobbes substitutes (in opposition to Aristotle) power for language, oppression for freedom, obedience for deliberation, uniformity for pluralism, subjects for citizens, market transactions for free speech, utilitarianism for public virtue, and the Sovereign's exclusive knowledge of the common good for politics.

The subsequent chapter illustrates how relative all talk about 'antipolitics' is, how dependent on prior notions of politics. In his extensive introductory remarks Erwin Jaffe speaks

up for rehabilitating Thomas Hobbes, against Weiler, as an
eminently 'propolitical' writer. Hobbes, he says, understood
that life without politics, in self-regulated, stateless societies, is
very likely to take an uncomfortable course, 'solitary, poor,
nasty, brutish and short'. And he continues arguing that in the
United States undercurrents of antipolitical thought have
been strong and pervasive since the nation's origins. The New
World's foundational egalitarianism and individualism as well
as other factors, such as the availability of empty space (which
implied the possibility to solve conflicts by simply moving on)
have, according to Jaffe, conspired to create a political culture
of contempt for politics. People imagine that society constitutes a self-sufficient, self-regulated, market-like order of free
individuals, and they regard politics as an unnecessary evil, as
mere 'politicking', that is, a particularistic, businesslike
exchange of favours among the political elite.

Charles Fairbanks undertakes a different journey than the
preceding authors. He travels east, namely to the successor
states of the former Soviet Union. The dark picture he paints
reads as another commentary on Hobbes, though without
mentioning him. The world he describes, which is a world not
so much of warring individuals than of warring tribes, resembles a communitarian version, an ethnopolitical update of
Hobbes's state of nature. *Natio nationi lupus est.* Where politics
once was omnipresent as well as oppressive, people now tend
to reject it as such. In this post-Leviathan realization of
Hobbes's pre-Leviathan negative utopia it is not just the state
but politics itself that is withering away. Public spaces, public
roles, public ethics, public obligations, public goals, all that
crumbles under the destructive dynamics of unleashed,
unbound individualism.

In her contribution Gwen Brown proceeds to analyze one
prominent antipolitical-establishment actor: H. Ross Perot.
After giving a brief chronological review of the 1992 US presidential campaign, she delivers an in-depth analysis of the
former (and perhaps future) presidential candidate's antipolitical discourse. Analysing both written and spoken texts
(television appearances, talk shows and televised debates) she
describes three basic *topoi*. First, Ross Perot identifies federal
public officials as the United States' 'problem number one'.
He describes 'the people in Washington' as being arrogant

and corrupt, incompetent and inefficient. Second, he portrays himself as an untainted outsider and radiant saviour. Third, he steps into politics as an 'action hero' who urges that something has to be done and done quickly. He demands less talk and more action. We know what we have to do, he claims, suggesting, as Gwen Brown puts it, that 'deliberation has already occurred'. In this respect her fears run parallel to Gershon Weiler's. She worries about the prospect of Ross Perot emerging, so to speak, as a postmodern Leviathan who replaces democratic deliberation with common sense plus technocratic enlightenment, with discretionary, solitary decisions and with managerial styles of action. She concludes by advancing the hypothesis that, after the disintegration of the Soviet Union, the 'antipolitical' construction of enemies appears to succeed, as a functional equivalent, to the invocation of the former communist enemy. In the new antipolitical rhetoric, the 'empire of evil' has moved its headquarters from Moscow to Washington.

Louis Pauly, the political economist, turns his attention to the relationship between politics and economics in an era of economic globalization. He concentrates on one crucial aspect, the spectacular growth in the international mobility of capital which has taken place especially since the late 1970s. From a neoliberal perspective, this process of capital market liberalization fulfils a rare condition of harmony. It combines the necessary with the desirable. Pauly puts this double assertion into question. On the one hand he rejects the 'language of inevitability' which treats the globalization of capital as an economic law of nature. He reminds us that capital decontrol, now masquerading as the evolutionary outcome of inescapable systemic forces, has been established through deliberate policy choices. It was politics itself which pursued and reinforced the primacy of the economic. On the other hand Pauly hints at the distressing political consequences the globalization of capital and the erosion of political control it provokes may produce. In spite of economic transnationalization, people continue to hold their national governments accountable for national economic performance. As Pauly argues, this gap between sovereignty and responsibility, this mismatch between power and attribution, creates problems of democratic legitimation, which may very well provoke 'anti-

political' responses. Pauly suggests that such reactions may be
of two opposite types. Offensive, pro-market, depoliticizing,
antistate, and non-nationalist movements (such as the
Canadian Reform Party or the Italian Lega Nord) welcome
economic transnationalization, while defensive, protectionist,
repoliticizing, statist and nationalist actors (such as Ross Perot
or European right-wing populists) combat it.

Norbert Lechner's 'cartographic' reflections on 'the changing cognitive maps of politics' are inspired by, but by no
means restricted to, Latin American experiences. The familiar
maps of modern politics, he states, are becoming anachronistic. Both its spatial and temporal boundaries are moving, blurring, vanishing. In the first, in the spatial dimension, the
acceleration and deepening of economic transnationalization
have led to a situation in which the capitalist economy escapes
the reach of national politics to an unprecedented extent. At
the same time, economic criteria of market exchange and
profit maximization have migrated into politics, subverting its
standards of public concern. Thus, with economics evading its
national logic and invading its public logic, the space of politics shrinks twice. In the temporal dimension, a similar contraction seems to be taking place. Politics' temporal horizon
tends to shorten. Losing its creative capacity, its presumptive
hold on the future, politics tends to become stuck in the
present, in the myopic administration of the here and now.
According to Lechner the cumulative impact of these structural changes amounts to a true epistemological crisis of
politics.

ACKNOWLEDGMENTS

The essays gathered in this book are all (some slightly, some
profoundly) revised versions of selected papers which were
originally presented in July 1994 at the First Vienna Dialogue
on Democracy on 'The Politics of Antipolitics', organized by
the Austrian Institute for Advanced Studies. At this point we
would like to express our gratitude to the sponsors who contributed to the success of this meeting: the Austrian National
Bank, the Commission of the European Union, the Austrian
Federal Chamber of Labour, the City of Vienna, the German

Friedrich Ebert Foundation, the Vienna Convention Bureau, and Raiffeisen Insurance. Thanks, too, to all participants who made the First Vienna Dialogue a socially as well as intellectually rich and stimulating experience. I also thank my colleagues Rainer Bauböck and Josef Melchior for their continual advice as well as Gertrud Hafner for her professionalism and dedication. Last but not least I want to thank my wife, Lina Cruz, whose patience was severely tested during the many evenings and weekends absorbed by the time-consuming conference and book preparations.

Notes

1. See G. J. Mulgan, *Politics in an Antipolitical Age* (Cambridge: Polity, 1994).

2. See, for example, H. Arendt, *On Revolution* (London: Penguin, 1963), pp. 19, 136; S. Berger, 'Politics and Antipolitics in Western Europe in the Seventies', *Daedalus*, vol. 108, no. 1 (1979), pp. 27–50; B. Crick, *In Defence of Politics*, 4th edn (London: Penguin, 1992), pp. 130–9; J. Citrin, 'Comment: The Political Relevance of Trust in Government', *The American Political Science Review*, vol. 68 (1974), p. 975; G. Konrád, *Antipolitik: Mitteleuropäische Meditationen* (Frankfurt/Main: Suhrkamp, 1985); A. Schedler, 'Anti-Political-Establishment Parties', *Party Politics*, vol. 2, no. 3 (1996), pp. 291–312.

3. See, for example, N. Luhmann, *Soziale Systeme* (Frankfurt/Main: Suhrkamp, 1987), pp. 513, 626; N. Luhmann, *Die Wirtschaft der Gesellschaft* (Frankfurt/Main: Suhrkamp, 1987), pp. 140–3, 150; N. Luhmann, *Paradigm Lost: Über die ethische Reflexion der Moral* (Frankfurt/Main: Suhrkamp, 1990), pp. 23–4.

4. See, for example, P. Bourdieu, *Sozialer Sinn: Kritik der theoretischen Vernunft* (Frankfurt/Main: Suhrkamp, 1987), p. 201.

5. See, for example, N. Luhmann, *Soziale Systeme*, op. cit.

6. Cf. Mulgan, op. cit., p. 26, or Crick, op. cit., pp. 123–30, though the latter does not speak of 'antipolitical' but 'apolitical' liberalism.

7. See J. M. Buchanan, 'Rent Seeking and Profit Seeking', in J. M. Buchanan, R. D. Tollison and G. Tullock (eds), *Toward a Theory of the Rent-Seeking Society* (College Station: Texas A&M University Press, 1980), pp. 3–15.

8. See H. Arendt, *Was ist Politik?* (München and Zürich: Piper, 1993), pp. 32–5; W. D. Narr, 'Politische Theorie wofür?', *Österreichische Zeitschrift für Politikwissenschaft*, vol. 18, no. 1 (1989), p. 78.

9. See Bourdieu, op. cit., p. 201; N. Elias, *Über die Zeit* (Frankfurt/Main: Suhrkamp, 1988) p. 16; H. Wimmer, *Evolution der Politik* (Vienna: WUV, 1996), chap. 3.

10. See, for example, I. Wallerstein, *The Modern World-System* (New York: Academic Press, 1974).

11. See, for example, U. Beck, *Die Erfindung des Politischen* (Frankfurt/Main: Suhrkamp, 1993); T. Meyer, *Die Transformation des Politischen* (Frankfurt/Main: Suhrkamp, 1994).
12. See, for example, A. Przeworski, 'The Neoliberal Fallacy', in L. Diamond and M. F. Plattner (eds), *Capitalism, Socialism, and Democracy Revisited* (Baltimore and London: Johns Hopkins University Press, 1993), pp. 39–53.
13. See D. Easton, *A Systems Analysis of Political Life* (New York: Wiley, 1965); H. Willke, *Ironie des Staates* (Frankfurt/Main: Suhrkamp, 1992), p. 45; Wimmer, op. cit.
14. See, for example, M. Weber, 'Politik als Beruf', 5th edn, in M. Weber, *Gesammelte Politische Schriften*, (ed.) Johannes Winckelmann (Tübingen: Mohr, 1988), p. 506.
15. See, for example, Arendt, op. cit., *On Revolution*, chap. 6.
16. T. Hobbes, *Leviathan* (Stuttgart: Reclam, 1970), chap. 13.
17. See, for example, J. Habermas, *Faktizität und Geltung* (Frankfurt/Main: Suhrkamp, 1992), p. 537.
18. See J. Dryzek, *Discursive Democracy* (Cambridge: Cambridge University Press, 1990); J. Fishkin, *Democracy and Deliberation* (New Haven and London: Yale University Press, 1991); Habermas, op. cit.; Meyer, op. cit.
19. Elsewhere I have distinguished four modes of democratic representation which may conflict with or complement each other: mandate, delegation, responsiveness and deliberation. See A. Schedler, 'Taking Electoral Promises Seriously: Reflections on the Substance of Procedural Democracy', paper presented at the 16th World Congress of the International Political Science Association (IPSA), Berlin, 21–5 August 1994. On consociational versus competitive types of democracy, see A. Lijphart, *The Politics of Accommodation: Pluralism and Democracy in the Netherlands* (Berkeley and Los Angeles: University of California Press, 1968); A. Lijphart, *Democracy in Plural Societies: A Comparative Exploration* (New Haven and London: Yale University Press, 1977). On consensual versus majoritarian democracy, see A. Lijphart, *Democracies: Patterns of Majoritarian and Consensus Government in Twenty-One Countries* (New Haven and London: Yale University Press, 1984).
20. S. M. Lipset and S. Rokkan, 'Cleavage Structures, Party Systems, and Voter Alignments: An Introduction', in S. M. Lipset and S. Rokkan (eds), *Party Systems and Voter Alignments: Cross-National Perspectives* (New York and London: Free Press, 1967), pp. 1–64.
21. J. Habermas, *Theorie des kommunikativen Handelns*, 2 volumes (Frankfurt/Main: Suhrkamp, 1982).
22. On images of the politician as doctor and mate, see H. Münkler, *Politische Bilder, Politik der Metaphern* (Frankfurt/Main: Fischer, 1994), pp. 125–40. See also Przeworski, op. cit.
23. J. Habermas, ibid.

2 Antipolitical Motifs in Western Political Discourse

Barry Hindess

Antipolitics sometimes takes the form of a rejection of the world of public affairs in favor of philosophy, religion, the contemplation of nature or some other field of activity. But there is also a more directly political antipolitics in which 'politics' as a means of conducting public affairs is condemned and some alternative way of conducting those affairs is proposed in its place. In these cases, a range of activities and institutions known as 'politics' is rejected in favor of what seems to be another kind of politics.

Far from representing a rejection of Western political culture, political antipolitics is one of its most familiar expressions. The combination of a negative perception of one kind of politics with a positive perception of another kind of politics has been a widespread feature of Western political discourse throughout the modern period. Madison's discussion in *The Federalist Papers* no. 10 clearly aims to protect the work of government from the politics of faction – in other words from the 'dangerous vice' that has since come to predominate in the USA and other Western democracies – but it is equally clearly committed to the defense of what he thinks of as popular government. Populist antipolitics, to take a rather different example, is also opposed to the politics of faction but, unlike the American Federalists who identify faction as 'number of *citizens*',[1] its animus is directed primarily against the factionalism of *politicians* and of parties. However even the most explicit populist contempt for politics is generally far from expressing a hostility to government as such. Rather its animus is directed against what it sees as the corruption of the proper conduct of government by 'politics'.

Both the American Federalists and populism seek to defend the proper conduct of government from what they would regard as damaging 'political' interference. However it would be a mistake to suppose that antipolitical standpoints always take such a view. Consider, for example, Foucault's comments on the political rationality which, he claims,

> has grown and imposed itself all throughout the history of Western societies. It first took its stand on the idea of pastoral power, then on that of reason of state. Its inevitable effects are both individualisation and totalisation. Liberation can only come from attacking, not just one of these two effects, but political rationality's very roots.[2]

Foucault's antipolitics are directed precisely against the political rationality that takes as its object the proper conduct of government. When Foucault invokes the idea of liberation in opposition to that of political rationality, the term 'political' itself is to be understood, not only in the sense of governmental but also, more specifically, as referring to what he sometimes describes as an 'autonomous' rationality of government – which is precisely what the American Federalists wished to defend against the impact of faction.

Even this limited sample of standpoints that are in some sense antipolitical is enough to show that there is no one 'politics' to which they are all opposed, and no alternative 'politics' of a kind that they all favor. In this respect it is difficult to generalize about the character of antipolitics. What these political antipolitical standpoints have in common is little more than the fact that they each distinguish between a politics they reject and another, antipolitical, politics that they favor – and the fact that they do so in terms of a positive or negative evaluation of some presumed 'autonomous' rationality of government.

This chapter examines the negative perceptions of politics invoked by antipolitical sentiments and the alternative positive perceptions of politics with which they are commonly associated in terms of the features of Western political discourse on which they depend. I argue that most if not all contemporary understandings of politics can be seen as based upon (or descended from) various metaphorical elaborations of the idea of politics as attending to the affairs of the *polis* or to the *res publica* – that is, they can be seen as derived from the ideal-ized representations of the public life of the cities of classical antiquity. What these idealizations share is an image of politics as the collective activity of a community consisting, at least in part, of autonomous political actors.

The contemporary development of antipolitical sentiments and movements can be considered in terms of two features of these idealizations. One is that the perception of politics as an activity of autonomous persons involves a corresponding view of a non-political domain. In fact the boundaries between these two domains have always been regarded as somewhat in-secure. As a result the political or governmental sphere has been thought to be in danger of corruption by the invasion of concerns that properly belong elsewhere, while the non-political domain has been thought to be in danger from the tyrannical reach of government. The decisive development for the appearance of antipolitics is the emergence of competing usages such that 'politics', in one sense of the term, can be denigrated in contrast with a non-political 'politics' of what seems to be a different kind. The perception of politics as open to corruption takes its characteristically modern form with the emergence in the early modern period of the idea of the state as a discrete set of institutions, separate from the person of the ruler of rulers. This development makes possi-ble a perception of 'politics' as a specialized kind of activity, not to be confused with other aspects of public life. It is a short step from this perception to the materialist understand-ing of politics, not as something that may be corrupted, but rather as an inescapably corrupt sphere of public activity. It is this understanding of politics that underlies the more extreme versions of the antipolitical dream of an ideal *polis* without politics.

However if antipolitics is a perpetual temptation of political discourse, some further explanation is clearly required of its current popularity. The last section of this chapter suggests reasons why the currency of many 'antipolitical' sentiments may have increased in recent years. The argument here turns on a second feature of the metaphor of the *polis* or *res publica*, namely that it presents an ideal image of the political commu-nity as culturally (and often 'racially') homogeneous and as having the capacity to govern itself. In practice, of course, the idea that a community could be entirely self-governing has always been regarded as something of a fantasy. However, significant developments in the contemporary world have further emphasized the disjunction between ideal image and mundane reality – the widespread loss of faith in the effectiveness of what might loosely be called 'Keynesian' economic management is an obvious example. Similar points may be made with regard to the ideal image of cultural homogeneity. To the extent that the activities of national governments are judged in terms of such ideal images (and are thus found wanting on many counts), we should not be surprised to find a reassertion of the importance of imaginary cultural and moral unities and a corresponding perception that 'politics' has failed.

THE METAPHOR OF THE POLIS

Let me begin, then, with the strict understanding of politics as the affairs of the *polis*. There is little scope here for the emergence of a clear distinction between the activity of government and political action which, in the more general sense suggested by Weber's definition, aims 'at exerting influence on the government of a political organization; especially at the appropriation, expropriation, redistribution or allocation of the powers of government'[3] – a distinction that is central to any political antipolitics. For the Greek citizens of the independent city-states – if not for those of the cities under Persian rule or of the later Hellenistic world – politics was simply the activity of collective self-government. This archaic identification of the political and the governmental clearly relies on the idea of the *polis* as a self-contained community of a very particular kind – that is, as a community consisting of individuals who are able to participate in the conduct of its affairs as autonomous agents.

   This is the sense of politics that Arendt intends to invoke when, in the opening pages of *The Human Condition*, she refers us to 'the Greek understanding of *polis* life, which to them denoted a very special and freely chosen form of political organization and by no means just any form of action necessary to keep men together in an orderly fashion'.[4]

Perhaps the most interesting feature of this passage is Arendt's reference to the idea of the *polis* as a 'freely chosen form of *political* organization' – a formulation which implies that there may also be forms of political organization that are not freely chosen in the appropriate sense. The identification of politics with the government of the *polis* suggests to Arendt, as it had to many others before her, an obvious extension to the government of other relatively self-contained communities that are regulated by laws – including customary laws – even if they have no equivalent to the collective self-governing activity of the kind that is thought to have been practiced by the citizens of the *polis*.[5] This last possibility gives us one of the senses in which it has often been thought possible to identify polities that are without real politics because their inhabitants are regarded either as unfree or else as unpolished, and therefore as governed by custom and tradition – in other words not by the collective decisions of citizens.[6]

I have already referred to Weber's proposal to treat as political that action which is oriented towards the conduct of government. To adopt this Weberian usage is to say, contrary to Foucault's usage noted above, that *political rationality* is not always to be identified with the rationality of government itself: it might also be concerned, for example, with the question of how best to influence the work of government or how best to take it over. Political action in this latter sense, action that is not necessarily governmental, is something that can be attributed only to members of a political community whose actions are regarded as being in some important degree free from direct government control – whose actions, in other words, are not themselves regarded as the actions of government. In the absence of tyranny the citizens of a *polis* will of course be free in the relevant sense. However, since the metaphor of the *polis* also suggests that citizens are both governors and governed, it will not necessarily lead to any clear distinction between the governmental and the political. This further step requires the emergence of a distinction between the action of government and the political action of free persons.

This development can take place in a number of ways. In classical antiquity, for example, the incorporation of a previously independent city within a larger empire clearly involved a level of government that was not reducible to the work of the citizens themselves. The crucial development in the modern period has been the gradual emergence in the cities of northern Italy of the conception of the state as a discrete set of institutions, distinct from the life of the ruler or rulers of the political community.[7] In fact this development makes possible two rather different perceptions of politics and the political. On the one hand there is the perception of the political, in the sense of governmental, as itself constituting a specialized field of activity, separable from other aspects of public life – and separable, in particular, from what later became known as 'civil society' or 'the economy'. On the other hand, especially where the rulers are also regarded as citizens, the concept of the state as a distinctive institutional structure nevertheless suggests that the public life of citizens is not reducible to the work of government, thereby giving rise to something approaching the Weberian understanding of politics as a sphere of activity that goes beyond the directly governmental.

This conception of the state also suggests a view of the ruled as comprising, at least in principle, a relatively stable population and territory – that is, as a territorial community existing independently of its subjection to some particular ruler or rulers. In this respect the development of the concept of the state can be seen as a precondition of those new forms of political rationality which Foucault sees emerging in parts of Western Europe during the seventeenth century: the concern for the welfare and security of the population – as distinct from, and sometimes in contrast to, that of the ruler; the generalization of discipline throughout society; and the governmental adoption of the model of pastoral power.[8] Here too the combination of the metaphor of the *polis* – or of the *res publica* – with the concept of the state gives a distinctive character to the conception of government: it is the government of a community consisting, *inter alia,* of at least some autonomous persons and having a political life that is not entirely subject to the government's (in other words the state's) control. Any such government will, of course, be subject to the impact of 'politics'.

THE PROBLEM OF CORRUPTION

While these points may suggest something of the diversity of modern understandings of 'politics', they can hardly account for the negative perceptions of 'politics' to be found in the various antipolitical standpoints of the modern period. Here, too, Arendt's discussions provide, if not an entirely reliable guide, then at least a useful reference point. In *The Human Condition* she claims to trace the modern denigration of politics back to its origins in the dualistic world view of the Greek philosophers. I have already referred to Arendt's description of 'the Greek understanding of *polis* life' as involving 'a very special and freely chosen form of political organization'.[9] A page or so later she insists that the devaluation of politics which locates it amongst the other pursuits of the necessities of life – rather than as a realm of free choice – can be found not only in early Christianity, but also in the works of Plato and Aristotle. The philosophers, in other words, 'added freedom and surcease from political activity' to 'the ancient freedom from the necessities of life and from compulsion by others'[10] and contrasted all of these with the life of contemplation.

As Arendt presents the story, this denigration of politics by the philosophers is the worm in the bud of Western civilization – so that, in spite of the recuperation of classical ideas after the European dark ages, the worm continued to munch away, finally emerging in the theoretical antipolitics of Marx and Nietzsche – and in the practical subordination of modern politics to other spheres of activity. While, in this view, the denigration of politics is present almost from the earliest appearance of politics itself, its full effects finally emerge only in the modern period.

Arendt's account is by no means entirely fanciful, but there are at least two distinct denigrations of politics that should be considered here. One follows directly from a dualistic contrast between a world of incorruptible truth and beauty on the one hand and the change and decay of the world of the senses on the other. Insofar as politics deals with the latter, it compares unfavorably with the life of contemplation. The affairs of the *polis* nevertheless remain, and they have to be dealt with.

There is nothing in the dualistic world-view to suggest the further denigration of politics itself in contrast with alternative means of dealing with these affairs – although it may be tempting to find this second denigration implied in the philosophers' argument that rule by philosophers is the best form of government. It is in this sense, for example, that Farrar[11] interprets Plato and Aristotle somewhat anachronistically, as representing an antipolitical position arising from fear of factionalism and disorder: politics is OK, but only within its proper limits. In effect Farrar presents Aristotle as putting forward an account of politics that, in the twentieth-century West, has resurfaced as the 'realist' theory of democracy – almost as if he were an American Federalist before his time.

Since this second denigration requires a prior distinction between politics and other aspects of the public life of the community, we should not expect to find much sign of it amongst the independent Greeks of the classical period. I have suggested that this distinction appears only when the understanding of politics as the collective activity of citizens coexists with an understanding of governmental politics in other terms – most particularly in the modern period, with at least a rudimentary notion of the state. Under such conditions the negative perception of politics in one sense is entirely compatible with the positive valuation of politics in another sense: the state may be contrasted unfavorably with the collective self-government of its citizens, while the factional politics of the people may be similarly contrasted with the autonomous rationality of the state.

The aspect of the metaphor of the *polis* that is particularly significant for this second denigration of politics concerns the presumption of a well-defined boundary between the life of the *polis* and a corresponding non-political domain – a boundary that is thought to mark out (at least for the citizens) 'a realm of personal efficacy, order, and relative equality'.[12] The point here is simply that what makes such a view of the personal efficacy of the citizens possible is that they are regarded as having a secure basis of existence from which to participate in the life of the *polis* as autonomous persons. This means, in particular, that they are seen as not being essentially subordinated to others or even to the *polis* itself – so that while they may be subject to the laws and to other decisions of the *polis*, they are nevertheless also regarded as retaining a considerable degree of independence. Government of the *polis*, if it is not to appear to be tyrannical, must be experienced by such persons both as kind of *collective* decision making and as a matter of *individual* self-government – with both the individual and the collective acknowledging the constraints imposed by the other. This, of course, is a familiar refrain in modern political thought.

This distinction between the public life of the citizens and other aspects of the life of their society is a major source of modern demarcations between public and private. The most important point to notice here, however, is that this distinction also sustains a markedly ambivalent perception of the *polis* and consequently of politics itself. Not only will there be different views as to where precisely the boundary between the political and the non-political should lie, but there will always be those who regard it as presently lying in the wrong place – and whatever boundary may be presumed to exist it can hardly be regarded as entirely secure.[13] On the one hand this suggests that the autonomy of the citizen may be perceived as being in danger of subversion – if not as already having been subverted – by political action. This is what is at issue when, shortly before the passage quoted in my opening discussion, Foucault refers to the state as a 'factor for individualisation'[14] – and it is also a recurrent theme in recent liberal and libertarian thought.

On the other hand the political sphere may be perceived as being in danger of corruption by the invasion of concerns that properly belong elsewhere. The problem here is seen as arising not so much from the existence of private concerns and interests, as from their improper intrusion into public life – an intrusion that is often seen as leading to what Locke calls tyranny, that is, to the expansion of governmental power into areas where it has no right to be. This, of course, is the dangerous propensity of popular government that Madison warns against in his discussion of faction in *The Federalist Papers* no. 10.

The perception of the political or governmental sphere as in danger of corruption turns on the presumption that there are activities and concerns that properly belong to this sphere and other activities and concerns that do not belong to it.

Where the political is itself understood in something like the Weberian sense – that is, in relation to an institutionally distinct state or government – this amounts to the view that there are activities and concerns that properly belong to the state and others that do not. To see what is at issue here it may be useful to turn to another of Foucault's lectures. In the opening sections of his 'Governmentality' lecture Foucault refers us to those anti-Machiavellian writers of the early modern period who aimed to distance themselves 'from a certain conception of the art of government which ... took the sole interest of the prince as its object and principle of rationality'.[15] In its place 'they attempted to articulate a kind of rationality which was intrinsic to the art of government, without subordinating it to the problematic of the prince and his relationship to the principality of which he is lord and master'.[16]

Their aim, in other words, was to articulate a *political* rationality that focused on the government of a state – as distinct from what might well, in another usage, be called the *political* rationality of the prince. Foucault therefore goes on to argue that, while the *idea* of an autonomous art of government is clearly present in this anti-Machiavellian literature, such an art could not be properly developed so 'long as the institutions of sovereignty were the basic political institutions and the exercise of power was conceived as an exercise of sovereignty'.[17] His suggestion, in other words, is that the political rationality of the prince or of his various surrogates – including 'the people' considered as a sovereign power – functioned as an obstacle to the development of an autonomous political rationality of government. For that development, Foucault maintains, we have to wait until the eighteenth century.

What should be noted here is the relationship between the idea that there is an 'autonomous' art of government and 'politics' in the Weberian sense noted above. In place of the political rationality of the prince in relation to the state that he wishes to rule, Weber invites us to consider as 'political' the rationality of the party or the movement – and, of course, of the individuals who seek to lead or to influence them. If the anti-Machiavellian exponents of the art of government established a sense in which the rationality of the prince could be seen as subverting the proper conduct of the business of government, so they also established an influential understanding of government which allowed the rationality of the party or movement to be similarly represented. In terms of this understanding of government we should expect to find that, whenever politics in the Weberian sense plays an important part in the life of the community, government is seen as being in danger of corruption by the rationality of faction.

This point returns us to the fundamental problem of institutional design set out in *The Federalist Papers*: how to reconcile popular government with a minimum of political interference in the autonomous rationality of government. Liberal discourse has always been concerned with the maximization of individual liberty and especially with the defense of such liberty against the state, but it has also been concerned with what it regards as the severely practical problem of defending the work of government from the corrupting effects of the political activity that such liberty makes possible. In this respect, liberalism might well be described as by far the most influential antipolitical doctrine of modern times.

The idea that there is or should be a clear distinction between the political and the non-political, then, suggests that the boundary is in danger of being crossed in both directions: that governments may act to subvert individual autonomy, that governments may be corrupted by the improper intrusion of private interests, or even that the two threats may be realized together – as in the notion of the tyranny of the majority. Such fears express an 'antipolitical' desire to bring politics under control and to protect it from bad habits – if only for its own good. The solution to these problems, however, can hardly be sought outside of 'politics' itself. Indeed the defense of the citizen from undue governmental interference and the defense of politics against corruption are both frequently regarded as amongst the central responsibilities of government. This leads to a further ironic twist to the tale of the liberal fear of governmental corruption. A liberal government will be concerned with defending the conduct of government from the impact of faction – and since any such government is likely to be corrupted by faction it will naturally be tempted to mobilize that concern for its own factional purposes. It will certainly be seen as having done so by its political opponents.

Finally, to conclude this section I should add that the significance of these boundary relations is further complicated by the development noted above of the modern idea of the state as a distinctive institutional form, and the corresponding view of politics as a specialized field of public activity, separable from other aspects of the public life of the community. Rather than an insecure distinction between the public life of the citizens and other aspects of the life of their community, we now have an equally insecure separation of at least three spheres: the governmental; the civil or public; and the private – with 'politics', in rather different senses, being seen as an integral part of the first two. Compared with the simple dichotomy, this more complex perception of distinct spheres provides scope for a greater variety of views as to the sources and consequences of corruption. In particular the state may be seen as imposing on and distorting the public life of the citizens, rather than reflecting their legitimate concerns; factional politics may be regarded as threatening the proper conduct of government; and both state and civil society may be seen as in danger of corruption by the intrusion of powerful sectional interests. Each one of these perspectives can sustain an antipolitical politics that aims to purge society of the corrupting impact of politics.

It is a short step from the last of these perspectives to the materialist understanding of politics not as something that may be corrupted, but rather as the corrupt reality itself.[18] From this perspective politics of whatever kind just *is* the pursuit of sectional interests, while the claim of disinterestedness will itself be seen as just another kind of corruption. I noted earlier that the metaphor of the *polis* suggests a sense in which there may be polities that are without politics. In the materialist understanding of politics the idea of a polity without politics takes the form of the twin romances popularized by Marxist socialism: primitive communism and advanced communism – human life before and after the corrupting effects of private property and the powerful interests that it generates.

THE FANTASY OF A SELF-GOVERNING COMMUNITY

However, to show how antipolitics could be regarded as a perpetual temptation of political discourse is to say little about the current popularity of antipolitical sentiments and movements in much of the world. It may not be difficult, of course, to understand negative perceptions of 'politics' on the part of those who are excluded from participation in the political process, but the emergence of significant antipolitical sentiments and movements under conditions of popular government appears somewhat paradoxical. What is particularly interesting about the current wave of antipolitics, then, is precisely its growth both in established democracies and in many democratising or recently democratized societies. The final section of this chapter focuses on one aspect of the metaphor of the *polis* that has a particular bearing on popular antipolitics in democratic societies. It concerns the notion of collective self-government, which supposes that the community has the capacity to exercise the control to which it makes claim. This is by no means the only influential conception of the capacities of government to be found in modern political discourse. My point is simply that it can be expected to be particularly influential whenever questions of government by the people or for the people are at issue.

'What happened in ancient Greece was that the sphere of communal life was wrested from the control of self-motivating processes and made subject to political action.'[19] Meier's formulation may be somewhat extreme but it clearly expresses an aspect of the understanding of politics in terms of the metaphor of the *polis* that bears strongly on our present discontents. This is the idea that, among the Greeks and for the first time in human history, the members of a community (or at least its citizens) were able to take control of their collective destiny. Such an idealized image of the *polis* sets a standard against which the mundane politics of other times and other places can be judged and generally found wanting.[20] In precisely this fashion, for example, Meier himself immediately goes on to maintain: 'Today, by contrast, political action itself has been overlaid with processes by which we ourselves – and our identity – appear to be motorized'.

Since the Athenian *polis* is commonly regarded as the birthplace of democracy, such expectations of politics have a particular pertinence for politics of a broadly democratic kind.[21] What is at stake here is nicely captured in Dahl's notion of final control over the agenda of government[22] – by which he means that all decisions affecting the life of the community should be made, if not always by the community itself, then at least by agencies and governing minorities that are regarded as answerable to the community. His point is not that all such decisions should in fact be made by the community or its government but rather that the community should be able to decide which of them should be brought under its direct control and which may safely be left to others. If it does not have that capacity, at least in principle, then the community of citizens can hardly be regarded as self-governing in the strong sense required by Meier's formulation or even by Dahl's more modest imagery.

Perhaps the most familiar difficulty with such an image of a self-governing community concerns the well-known tension in liberal democratic politics between a commitment to individual liberty on the one side and the aim of final control over the agenda of government on the other. Where the latter suggests that there can be no limits to the ends that government might choose to pursue, the former insists that the rights of individual citizens set limits to the actions of government. This conflict is a significant component of the American Federalists' problem of institutional design referred to above: how to achieve popular government by means of political arrangements that inhibit the domination of government by faction – which Madison describes as a group of citizens bound together by an 'interest, adverse to the rights of other citizens, or to the permanent and aggregate interests of the community'.[23]

A significantly different case for limited government derives from a perception of the political community as constituting an entity with a life of its own – an 'economy' or a 'society' – subject to its own identifiable laws and functional requirements that set a supposedly objective limit to what can realistically be placed on the agenda of government. Political economy and its successor, economics, have been by far the most successful exponents of this perspective, insisting that if government intervenes in the working of the economy, it should at least operate within constraints given by the nature of economic activity itself. Closely related arguments have been developed with respect to the idea of civil society and to the understanding of culture involved in the sense of self-government. What is at stake in all these cases is that an aspect of the life of the community is regarded as a primary source of the moral and other standards that regulate market and other types of social interaction without, as Hayek puts it, 'deliberate organization by a commanding intelligence'.[24] From this perspective there is always the danger that governmental interference in the working of the economy, in civil society or in culture will undermine the normative conditions on which orderly social interaction is thought to depend.

There is a perpetual conflict then between, on the one hand, expectations generated by the idea of final control of the agenda of government and, on the other, perceptions of both the normative and the practical limits to government. The 'practical' limits are the ones that concern me here. It is tempting to suggest that these limits have become more consequential in recent years for two reasons: firstly as the internationalization of trade and finance and the widespread deregulation of financial markets have undermined the broadly Keynesian view of national economic management that once was shared by social democratic parties and many of their political opponents on the right; and secondly as a result of the associated movements of people, artifacts, lifestyles and so on – in short, of things that cannot be regulated effectively at a national level without seriously undermining what remains of our political freedoms (and perhaps not even then). Nevertheless, it may be more realistic to suggest that what these developments have really undermined is a matter not so much of capacities that governments in the more prosperous societies of the modern West might once have possessed as of a set of expectations regarding those capacities that were once widely shared – at least in those societies.

Be that as it may, what matters for the present argument is that, while matters of economic management have an undeniable political importance, the widespread loss of faith in the ability of governments to manage affairs within their own societies is by no means confined to the economic sphere. On the one hand supranational agencies together, for much of Europe, with a supranational political community operate as an external constraint on what might otherwise be regarded as the sovereign freedom of many national governments. On the other hand the movement of people, narcotics, cultural artifacts and distinctive lifestyles across national boundaries have served both to threaten the ability of governments to manage their own affairs and to weaken the perception of the national community as a cultural and moral unity. We should not be surprised to find that reassertion of the importance of imaginary cultural and moral unities is a common response to the perceived incapacity of national governments either to provide economic security or to control the influx of alien persons and lifestyles.

CONCLUSION

How do these concerns with the governmental capacities of the political community relate to the antipolitical themes considered in the first two sections of this chapter? I argued there that most if not all contemporary understandings of politics could be seen as derived from idealized representations of the public life of the cities of classical antiquity. As a result they are commonly infected by concerns over the boundaries between the political and the non-political – and in particular by the fear that politics will be corrupted through the intrusion of extraneous elements and that politics itself will tend to corrupt other aspects of the life of the community. Since, especially in the modern period, the terms 'politics' and 'political' may refer both to the specialized work of government and to a realm of public activity that aims 'at the appropriation, redistribution or allocation of the powers of government',[25] it is not difficult to understand how on the one side 'politics' could be represented as threatening to corrupt government in particular nor on the other side how government, and even 'politics' more generally, could be regarded as subverting the life of the community.

The fear of corruption represents a concern not only that politicians will use their position for their own benefit, but also and more fundamentally that they will do so to the detriment of others. This is what lies behind the American Federalists' definition of faction as a group of citizens bound together by interests 'adverse to the rights of other citizens, or to the permanent and aggregate interests of the community'.[26]

The corruption of politics is perceived as a primary cause of its failure – and as leading in particular to government not doing what it should and also doing what it should not. Conversely governmental failure is easily represented as *prima facie* evidence of political corruption. This last temptation will be particularly strong if the performance of government is measured against the expectations of democratic politics considered above.

There is little that is new, of course, either in the perception that government has failed to manage the economy as well as it should or in the view that much of that failure should be seen as resulting from the corruption of government by 'politics' – but, with the partial exception of a few countries in western Europe and the Americas, it has usually been possible to attribute such failures to a politics that excluded important sections of the population. Following the recent victories of democracy in much of the world, it is now more difficult to appeal to the remedy of a more inclusive political system. Popular antipolitics is now directed against what is perceived to be the corruption of democracy by 'politics' or against democracy itself. Since an international economy that is beyond the control of any national government will be with us for the foreseeable future, it will continue to pose problems for influential understandings of what the collective self-government of 'the people' should be able to deliver. In these respects, then, there will continue to be ample scope for those who advance the antipolitical claim that government by the people has not lived up to its promise.

Notes

1. J. Madison, A. Hamilton and J. Jay (eds) *The Federalist Papers*, (ed.) Isaac Kramnick (London: Penguin, 1987; 1st ed. 1788), no. 10, emphasis added.
2. M. Foucault, 'Omnes et Singulatim: Towards a Criticism of Political Reason', S. McMurrin (ed.), *The Tanner Lectures on Human Values*, vol. 2 (Salt Lake City: University of Utah Press, 1981), p. 254.
3. M. Weber, *Economy and Society: An Outline of Interpretive Sociology* (Berkeley: University of California Press, 1978), p. 55.
4. H. Arendt, *The Human Condition* (Chicago: University of Chicago Press, 1958), p. 13.
5. A once influential example is Morgan's argument that all forms of government 'are reducible to two general plans.... The first, in the

order of time, is founded upon persons, and upon relations purely personal ...' The second, of course, is 'political society [which] deals with property as well as with persons through territorial relations'. L. H. Morgan, *Ancient Society* (New York: Meridian Books, 1963), pp. 6–7. This idea of an early form of government without politics was taken up by Friedrich Engels in *The Origin of the Family, Private Property and the State* and by many later Marxists – at one time including the present author. See B. Hindess and P. Q. Hirst, *Pre-Capitalist Modes of Production* (London: Routledge, 1975), chap. 1.

6. Finley's decision to exclude Rome under the emperors from his otherwise valuable discussion of politics in the ancient world is an instructive recent example of the first case. His decision rests on the claim that there can be no politics under conditions in which *'binding decisions'* are not 'reached by discussion and argument and ultimately by voting' but can in fact be made by one person. See M. Finley, *Politics in the Ancient World* (Cambridge, Mass.: Cambridge University Press, 1983), p. 52. An example of the second case is Meier's insistence that, while *the political* may be an ubiquitous feature of human existence, there was no real *politics* before its discovery by the Greeks. See C. Meier, *The Greek Discovery of Politics* (Cambridge, Mass.: Harvard University Press, 1990).

7. Q. Skinner, 'The state' in T. Ball, J. Farr and R. L. Hanson (eds), *Political innovation and conceptual change* (Cambridge: Cambridge University Press, 1989), pp. 90–131.

8. M. Foucault, *Discipline and Punish* (London: Penguin, 1979); M. Foucault, 'Omnes et Singulatim: Towards a Criticism of Political Reason', op. cit.; M. Foucault, 'Governmentality', in G. Burchell *et al.* (eds), *The Foucault Effect* (Chicago: University of Chicago Press, 1991), pp. 87–104.

9. Arendt, op. cit., p. 13.

10. Ibid., p. 14.

11. C. Farrar, *The Origins of Democratic Thinking: The Invention of Politics in Classical Athens* (Cambridge, Mass.: Cambridge University Press, 1988); C. Farrar, 'Ancient Greek Political Theory as a Response to Democracy', in J. Dunn (ed.), *Democracy: The Unfinished Journey 508 BC to AD 1993* (Oxford: Oxford University Press, 1992).

12. Farrar, op. cit., p. 18.

13. Farrar, for example, cites (and disputes) the Greek view that the *polis* boundary between citizen and non-citizen on the one hand and between the political and the non-political life of citizens on the other cannot ensure the exclusion of 'the primitive, the chaotic, the visceral (the slavish and womanish) from civic life' (ibid., p. 29).

14. M. Foucault, 'Omnes et Singulatim', op. cit., p. 254.

15. Ibid., p. 89.

16. Ibid.

17. Ibid., p. 97.

18. Compare the treatment of changing perceptions of politics in the early modern period in M. Viroli, *From politics to reason of state: The*

acquisition and transformation of the language of politics, 1250–1600 (Cambridge: Cambridge University Press, 1992).
19. Meier, op. cit., p. 6.
20. B. Hindess, 'Imaginary presuppositions of democracy', *Economy and Society*, vol. 20, no. 2 (1991), pp. 173–95.
21. Many commentators take the stronger view that there is an intimate connection between the birth of politics and the origins of democracy. Farrar and Meier are particularly clear recent examples.
22. R. A. Dahl, *Democracy and Its Critics* (New Haven and London: Yale University Press, 1989), especially chap. 8.
23. *The Federalist Papers*, no. 10.
24. F. A. Hayek, *The Constitution of Liberty* (London: Routledge, 1960), p. 159.
25. Weber, op. cit., p. 55.
26. *The Federalist Papers*, no. 10.

3 Logos against Leviathan: The Hobbesian Origins of Modern Antipolitics

Gershon Weiler

The manifest enmity of Thomas Hobbes to Aristotle is among the very first impressions the reader gets on reading *Leviathan*.[1] Aristotle is mentioned over and over again and to him are attributed, by proxy as it were, not only the things he actually said but also all that Hobbes objected to and detested about scholasticism and about those false and harmful political doctrines which, as he argued, it engendered. In contrast Plato is mentioned only few times and without any substantial reference to the contents of his philosophy. This is all the more surprising as Hobbes, in one of the few passing mentions of Plato, refers to him as 'the best philosopher of the Greeks'.[2] That the scarcity of references to Plato masks a deep affinity and indebtedness to Plato has not gone unnoticed. Leo Strauss, in his classic book on Hobbes,[3] devotes much space to an exposition of Hobbes's Platonism. According to Strauss, what Hobbes learnt from Plato was that political science ought to be an exact science.[4]

> The most profound expression which Hobbes finds for the differences between Plato and Aristotle is that Plato's philosophy starts from ideas, and Aristotle's from words....[5]
> What Hobbes's political philosophy owes to Platonism is, its antithetic character, the constituent conception of the antithesis between truth an appearance ... in the most extreme formulation, between reason and passion.[6]

To put the case in a nutshell, what Strauss is saying is that Hobbes admired and adopted Plato's antiempiricism, his refusal to argue from the contingent and his insistence that no political regime is worthy of support unless it is rationally justifiable *in toto*. The contrast between ideas and words is but the contrast between exact scientific concepts and what people say and will say, on occasion, as they conduct their lives. This dismissal of ordinary concepts in favor of more exact notions arrived at through stipulative and theory-bound definitions is typical of rigorous metaphysical systems; Spinoza too had a poor opinion of the kinds of things people say on no better ground than mere life experience. Hegel also thought poorly of the so-called *gesunder Menschenverstand*.[7]

Hobbes's *Leviathan* opens with long lists of would-be scientific definitions, chiefly of mental concepts. My guess is that the purpose of these definitions is not merely to construct a concept of man, as the title of the first part of the book indicates, which shall be fully fitted to bear the burden of Hobbes's political theory but also shake his readers' confidence in the one area where they might well believe that they know best because they have first-hand experience of it: their innermental life. As in any such enterprise, Hobbes's effort is directed towards clearing away common notions as fundamentally mistaken, and to pronounce truth, no matter how paradoxical it may appear.

Hobbes's political theory is a theory of security and as such it deligitimates all and any notions which are not fully subservient to it.[8] Like all single-minded theorists, Hobbes too brands as uncomprehending and ignorant all who do not grasp the central and overriding importance of his own favored concept, security. It is this core of Hobbes's philosophy which must be kept in mind throughout the brief survey of his critique of Aristotle, which I intend to present now. It is the purpose of this survey, as of my whole effort in this chapter, to show that what Hobbes found most objectionable in Aristotle is that his philosophy sanctioned political activity and that, by implication, when Hobbes rejected (in agreement with Plato) the legitimacy of such an activity, he in fact followed Plato in his antipolitics; as the first modern political philosopher, he inaugurated modern antipolitics in its most important varieties. The central characteristic of the Aristotelian notion of political activity is the general idea that it cannot be pursued without *logos*, speech, in other words discussion in the public space. Hobbes held, with Plato, that such discussions are harmful since they aid and promote to power the ignorant and thus ultimately create only trouble.

Hobbes's systematic critique of Aristotle, apart from the many remarks which occur frequently against 'Aristotelity',[9] is to be found in chapter 46 of *Leviathan*. I shall ignore here his criticisms of Aristotelian physics and shall outline briefly only what he has to say about ethics and politics. This part of Hobbes's attack opens thus: 'Aristotle, and other Heathen Philosophers define Good, and Evill by the Appetite of men. But in a Commonwealth this measure is false'.[10] Note that the objective of this criticism is to limit drastically the range of applicability of private judgement. When turning from ethics to the 'Civill Philosophy' of Aristotle,[11] Hobbes lists the errors of that philosophy. The first of these is Aristotle's well-known classification of forms of government: 'From Aristotles Civill Philosophy, they have learned, to call all manner of Common-wealths but the Popular *Tyranny*'.[12] The Hobbesian objection here is that by appending that name to some regimes they foster *hatred* of that regime, without understanding that tyranny is just monarchy which, *qua* government, is necessary for the maintenance of public safety. And then comes the register of other errors in Aristotle's political philosophy: 'And therefore this is another Error of Aristotles Politiques, that in a well-ordered Common-wealth, not Men should govern, but the Laws'. Why this is such a bad error is simple enough: 'And this is of the number of pernicious Errors: for they induce men, as oft as they like not their Governors, to adhere to those that call them Tyrants, and to think it lawful to raise warre against them'.[13]

And lastly there comes 'another error in their Civill Philosophy (which they never learned from Aristotle, nor Cicero, nor any other of the Heathen)',[14] and yet Hobbes clearly relates it to the errors of Aristotelian philosophy. This error, which indeed could not have begun until the advent of Christianity, is that thoughts, and not only actions, are subject to law and its retributions. This relates to one more error: 'For a Private man, without the authority of the Common-wealth, that it to say, without the permission of the Representant thereof, to interpret the Law by his own Spirit, is another error of the Politiques; but not drawn from Aristotle...'[15]

It seems to me that this exoneration of Aristotle is pedantic for the substance of the criticism. That the scholastics teach that man is free to interpret the laws is intimately related to the error which Hobbes clearly attributes to Aristotle, to wit, that government is not by men but laws. The crux of the matter is that if supremacy is vested in laws and not in rulers, then inevitably there must be some public thinking about the laws. There must be some procedures which determine what the meaning of the law is and how it applies in particular cases. Neither of these objectives can be attained without discussion and it is this, I submit, to which Hobbes most objects in Aristotelian political philosophy. For, as we have seen the consequence of such discussion might be the worst result of all, from a Hobbesian point of view. Subjects may rise against their tyrants, rulers who govern as men without the constraints of law. This is why Hobbes wishes to outlaw the very use of the term 'tyrant'; its very presence in the vocabulary is a sort of permanent incitement. Needless to say, Hobbes was fighting no phantom but a very real enemy. Aristotle's listing of tyranny as the worst of the corrupt form of regimes became a practical ruling at the hands of Saint Thomas: 'Among unjust governments, therefore, democracy is the most tolerable, but the worst is tyranny'.[16] Consequently, Aquinas also taught that tyrants may be deposed,[17] although he was careful to set limits, as far as such remedial action is concerned, to the 'private presumptions of the few'.[18] It was this continuous antityranny tradition which finally emerged in the famed *Vindiciae Contra Tyrannous.*[19] It was a tradition highly active at the time Hobbes wrote[20] and Hobbes knew its dangers for his type of conception of sovereignty. Therefore, quite consistently, amidst the ongoing debate of his time about *what* was the right interpretation of the laws of England, he insisted that it did not matter; the real question was *who* was doing the interpreting.[21]

Hobbes's attack on Aristotle's errors should be read in conjunction with chapter 29, 'Of those things that Weaken, or tend to the dissolution of a Commonwealth'. Here too the reader will find a list of ailments which are dangerous to the state, not the least of which is 'the Liberty of Disputing against absolute power, by pretenders to Political Prudence.'[22] Hobbes is aware, of course, that no system of government can work without speech between rulers and subjects. But he does not take this speech to be in the nature of *logos*, discussion where *public*, though not scientific, criteria are available to determine who is right and who is wrong,[23] for it is discussion as such which is the root of all evil. Rather, Hobbes designates the speech necessary between rulers and subjects as being in the nature of *public instruction* by the sovereign and to which the response of the subject is to be, like the conclusion of an Aristotelian practical syllogism, obedient action. Hobbes's discourse of public instruction is to be found in chapter 30 of *Leviathan*, the title of which is 'The office of the Sovereign Representative'. The Sovereign is here not only the ruler but also the supreme Teacher of his subjects.

> [I]t is his Duty, to cause them so to be instructed.... And ... the People are to be taught, First that they ought not to be in love with any form of Government they see in their neighbor Nation.... Secondly ... that they ought not to be led with admiration of the virtue of any of their fellow Subjects.... Thirdly, ... they ought to be informed, how great a fault it is, to speak evill of the Sovereign Representative.... Fourthly ... it is necessary that some such times be determined, wherein they may assemble together, and ... hear those their Duties told them, and the Positive Laws.... Again, every Sovereign Ought to cause Justice to be taught.... Lastly, they are to be taught, that not only the unjust facts, but the designs, and intentions to do them ... are injustice.[24]

I shall not go into the details of the seeming inconsistency of Hobbes to be found in the last sentence of this quotation. Only a few pages back we saw him condemning as an error the idea that not only deeds but also thoughts can be at fault, but then it would be easy for Hobbes to retort that the Sovereign as Public Instructor is not pronouncing theoretical truths but exhorting his subjects, by speech-acts he considers efficacious, to be obedient.[25] Rather we should pay attention to the similarity of this catalogue of things to be taught to subjects in order to make them obedient, to contemporary sorts of indoctrinations. In all these activities there is a lot of speech (how could it be otherwise?), but none of it is in the character of free exchange. That there ought to be no free discussion of matters politic is one of the cornerstones of Hobbesian antipolitics and this is his legacy to those of our contemporaries who would arrange our lives without giving us a say in it.

The philosophical underpinning of this stance is performed by two supports. One is Hobbes's view of philosophy, including the philosophy of politics. The other is his conception of virtue. And both are, as I shall try to indicate in what follows, in conscious opposition to Aristotle.

The idea that philosophy, including practical philosophy, in other words ethics and politics, is an exact science, excludes from consideration and denies the right of having an opinion, even at first blush, to all those who are not learned in it. It is well known that Aristotle carefully distinguished the theoretical from the practical sciences, thus allowing in the latter a solid foothold for human experience and for whatever measure of practical wisdom the individual is capable of attaining as a consequence of it. All Aristotle has to say about the virtues, and especially about practical wisdom, is incomprehensible without the support of the typical life experience of the people he spoke to. Not so for Hobbes. 'By Philosophy, is understood the Knowledge acquired by Reasoning.... By which Definition it is evident, that we are not to account as any part thereof, that original knowledge called Experience, in which consisted Prudence: Because it is not attained by Reasoning.'[26]

If ordinary people's typical experience counts for nothing in politics, as indeed it does not in all those cases where they cannot do without experts, then in politics too they are in need of experts. This was Plato's view and Hobbes adopts it but with an interesting twist. The Platonic ruler had to pass the course of education prescribed in the *Republic* before he was qualified to rule; for Hobbes there are no such qualifying criteria, it is enough if he actually holds power and rules effectively. For Plato the philosopher is qualified to rule by his universal knowledge; for Hobbes it is enough if the ruler performs effectively, but it is not necessary for him to understand the philosophy which correctly expounds why he is ruler. It is better, of course, if the Sovereign understands that he is absolute, what his teaching office is, and so on. But it is enough if he performs well.[27]

Yet there is a role for knowledge in Hobbes. It logically must be, if there is to be public instruction. There must be something which is taught. That content of instruction is the simple message that the subject must obey the Sovereign in exchange for being protected by him. 'The Obligation of Subjects to the Sovereign, is understood to last as long, and no longer, than the power lasted, by which he is able to protect them.'[28] This is the famed 'obedience in exchange for protection' principle that Carl Schmitt made into the core not only of his interpretation of Hobbes[29] but also into one of the centerpieces of his whole political philosophy and the chief plank in his quasi-apology for his Nazi past.[30] We could read Hobbes here as democratizing, as it were, Platonic political knowledge, with the obvious difference that there is no need here to go to the academy and get good marks in the class of dialectics; it is sufficient if the subject understands that the Sovereign protects his life and that *therefore* he owes obedience to him. This is a very simple lesson and it is antipolitics reduced to its bare bones. There are no ideals here, no room for demands for justice (since justice for the subject is nothing but obedient performance),[31] no permission for thinking about and promoting alternative ways of life and so on. No discussion at all. The purpose of the state is clear and simple; everyone, even Lenin's cook,[32] should be able to understand it.

I just mentioned Carl Schmitt, certainly one of the most fascinating exponents of twentieth-century antipolitics. His views have changed over a very long and tumultuous career but he never wavered on the point that politics has nothing to do with discussion, that discussion is harmful and disruptive. Following the Spanish philosopher Juan Donoso-Cortes, he contemptuously referred to the bourgeoisie as the 'discussing class'.[33] I would go as far as to say that the attitude to discussion, *qua* the core of politics, is the dividing line which separates those who believe in politics from those who espouse antipolitics, regardless of the specific variety. This criterion neatly arrays Plato and Hobbes on the side of antipolitics as against Aristotle and others whose political theory is incomprehensible without discussion occupying a central role in it. And it is worth noting that it makes no difference, from this point of view, that Plato and Hobbes are so very different, that Plato's concept of unified knowledge expresses one of the top human aspirations of all times and that Hobbes's notion of political knowledge is plainly individualistic, indeed egoistic. One pursues the 'good', the other merely safety; neither has room for that activity which made the *polis* what it was and Aristotle its philosopher.

At this point it easy to see the relation between the concept of virtue and political conceptions of antipolitics. Plato taught us, in dialogue after dialogue, that the nature of justice, beauty, courage or religious piety is ultimately not comprehensible without universal knowledge and that these ideas are ultimately reducible, must be reduced, to knowledge. One cannot be courageous without *knowing* the difference between things that ought to be feared and those which need not. One cannot be just without the knowledge of justice. And so on. Hobbes too, as we have seen, reduces political virtue to one, or more precisely to two, one for the Sovereign, one for the subjects. The virtue of the Sovereign is his actual capacity to exercise control,[34] and the virtue of the subject is obedience. As is well known, Aristotle let ruling and obeying alternate in the state: '[T]he good citizen ought to know how to govern like a freeman, and how to obey like a freeman'.[35] Political virtue is the virtue of the free citizen.

The simplicity of virtue is a barrier to discussion and thus to political life. This life is an ongoing activity of speech and deed within which *not only means but also ends* are, as the need arises, subjected to examination and reexamination. Typically, systems of government which have a one-eyed view of final ends (Lenin's cook!) do now wish to allow such reexaminations. Recall that in the defunct Soviet Union even mentioning the idea that capitalism may be a better economic system amounted to a criminal offense. But there are other examples as well. Maimonides (1135–1204), the great medieval Jewish scholastic, was a rigorous Aristotelian in all but in his political philosophy. There he chose to be Platonic because it served him better in justifying unquestioning obedience to God's Law, the Torah, and in outlawing discussion about ultimate principles.[36]

The simplicity of virtue does not necessitate perplexities, choices and *painful* decisions. Of course it may still cause them in the unpredictable circuits of individual minds, but within one-virtue systems such contingencies are treated as unforeseen temporary breakdowns or individual failures but not, not ever, as things which follow from the imperfections of the system.

The antidote to Platonic or Hobbesian monism is, as indicated by now more than once, Aristotle. I shall now try to
show how his conception of virtue logically demands a conception of politics which entails discussion. In the first book of
the *Nichomachean Ethics* Aristotle takes up the problem of ends.
Why are we doing things and what things are worth doing?
Right at the beginning of the book he says that the 'master
art', the science of the *good* for man, is politics.[37] He then goes
on to the problem of what that good actually is and soon
comes to the conclusion that the end which is never instrumental is happiness, the flourishing of the human being, in
his term: *eudaimonia*. But, and this is really an astonishing
thing, Aristotle does not conceive this final end the same way
as Plato conceives knowledge or Hobbes safety. Quite the contrary, he notes, obviously relying on human experience and
linguistic usage, that *eudaimonia* is not an *exclusive* final end;
there are others as well.

> Now we call that which is itself worthy of pursuit more final
> than that which is worthy of pursuit for the sake of some-
> thing else.... Now such a thing happiness [*eudaimonia*],
> above all else, is held to be; for this we choose always for
> itself and never for the sake of something else, but honour,
> pleasure, reason, and every virtue we choose indeed for
> themselves (for if nothing resulted from them we should
> still choose each of them), but we choose them also for the
> sake of happiness, judging that by means of them we shall
> be happy. Happiness, on the other hand, no one chooses
> for the sake of these, nor, in general, for anything other
> than itself.[38]

This is a passage to which no justice can be done within the
limits of this chapter. But for our purposes it is sufficient to
note that, according to it, although the different virtues
promote happiness, *we choose honor, pleasure, reason and every
virtue for themselves*. It follows that the relationship between the
virtues, all of them, and *eudaimonia*, is not one of means and
ends. The virtues too are ends and not merely intermediate
instrumental ends: we choose those too for their own sake.
Now the kind of life which is reflected in this pluralistic image
of all sorts of virtues being chosen and acted upon in the
context of a general aspiration to flourish is very much recog-

nizable as the sort of life we know, the life of decent people, with reflective minds and good habits, who advance through their years by picking their way among difficult choices, hard predicaments, as these arise, always trying to strike the best balance between the demands of *conflicting virtues*. The idea that life is a totality harmonious with the universe and that all that spoils this harmony is human misdeeds only intends to prepare the way to the injunction that we should rigidly follow some code of behavior which is, according to its promoters, the human key to harmony.[39] That sort of optimism typically surfaces in various systems of politics, religion and philosophy,[40] and in its extreme version denies the existence of bad things in the world altogether or at least denies them an intellectually respectable hearing.[41] But luckily we are not defenseless against such fraudulent wares. The tradition of tragedy and the Aristotelian philosophy are strong prophylactics against all versions of such absurdity, which may range from cheap optimism to chiliastic insanity. Tragedy and Aristotle tell us that life is hard and that it is not always sufficient to strive to be a good man, and even if outside forces do not overwhelm us, we might still fail because we did not think hard enough and made the wrong choices. It is not easy, and sometimes terribly difficult, to find one's way among many, equally demanding, virtues. But to deny their plurality is an all too easy way out.

The significance of this plurality of ends for politics, the master art, with the predicaments concomitant with it, cannot be overrated. For it simply teaches us that there are no wizards to tell us what to do, that the Platonic model of the physician, who always knows better than the patient what is good for the patient, just does not apply in politics. It tells us that in order to do well we need the help of others in sorting out our difficulties and that the minds of free citizens joined in a public effort to solve political problems is the best method available to attain the end of doing well. We need a constant awareness of the many-sidedness of the situations we find ourselves in. And what better source could there be for fostering this awareness than our fellow citizens who, although they see things from a different angle, and often precisely because they do so, are still our friends. Aristotle speaks scathingly of the Spartans who think that 'highest goods ... are to be obtained

by the practice of a single excellence'.[42] The Spartans were not
alone in extolling a single virtue at the expense of the complexity of life. Hobbes is a strikingly interesting philosopher
in this context. However, no matter how wrong he might have
been and irrespective of how much we may dislike his ideas,
Hobbes was a philosopher of the first order. It is a mark of his
greatness that he correctly identified and chose to argue
against the strongest opponent he could find. Not for
nothing, we now see, did Hobbes attack Aristotle, and moreover, from his point of view, he was right in assailing the
Aristotelian pluralism of virtues with its concomitant endorse-
ment of discussion as the essence of the most rational politics
available to human beings.

For Hobbes the individual was first, and it was the safety of
the individual which justified his subjection to an absolute
sovereign: protection in exchange for obedience. In this exchange Hobbes also surrendered the right of the individual to
action. For Aristotle a free citizen is marked by *logos* and *praxis*,
by the joint attributes of speech, common deliberation and
discussion in the public space. In contrast the obedient person
à la Hobbes speaks in public only when he is allowed to do so
and only to the extent to which the sovereign does not
object.[43] Speech as one's own autonomous action is true
public action, and therefore, in Hobbes, it is the exclusive
prerogative of the sovereign representative whose will is, in the
commonwealth, the measure of right and wrong. The would-
be liberty of subjects of 'disputing against absolute power' is,
as we saw above, one of infirmities of the state and, if it is bad
enough, it can be fatal for it.

But this quasi-totalitarian reading of Hobbes does not at all
exhaust the wealth of his philosophy. Hobbes is also the father
of utilitarianism and as such is our outstanding contemporary
from yet another point of view. If the state is there to protect
the individual then it exists for the benefit of the individual;
that subjects should understand this elementary truth is the
aim of public teaching. It follows that the individual stands in
a calculatory relationship to the state; the rational subject is
expected to calculate how far it is worthwhile to obey his (or
her) Sovereign.[44] By thinking this way Hobbes decisively
rejected aristocratic–heroic virtue[45] in favor of calculatory and
commercial attitudes. And although this sort of attitude has

gone in history, as a matter of fact, hand in hand with the institutions of more or less liberal democracies, there is an ineradicable element of antipolitics in it all the same. If the state is but an artifice created solely for the sake of its beneficiaries but without having any intrinsic value of its own then, again, politics becomes problematic, perhaps unjustified, as an autonomous activity.[46] The Founding Fathers of America were, at this point too, astonishingly farsighted, for they understood that a merely self-seeking population, without republican virtues, would not be capable of sustaining the Union.

The problem is not new and already almost a century ago it was explicitly raised by the great political philosopher Figgis in the very last sentences of his masterly work on the divine right of kings, where he noted that obedience must be 'enshrined in the hearts of the governed' for 'laws are vain without loyalty'. And then, looking into the future, in other words our present, he said this: 'Nor is it all clear that the widespread popular acceptance of a purely utilitarian basis for obedience may not lead to great dangers in the future.'[47]

Present-day politics shows an uncanny convergence of the two branches of political thought that have come forth from the Hobbesian root. Totalitarianism and utilitarianism, while in many ways antagonistic to each other, still display an affinity which testifies to their common source. It is not so long ago that we heard Nazi or socialist totalitarianism to be justified by the economic benefits it bestows on its subjects. Five-year plans were supposed to outdo selfish entrepreneurs in satisfying selfish needs and this was perhaps the most important ingredient in the rhetoric of communism, at any rate in those places where it was still compelled to fight for political power. The common enemy of both totalitarianism and utilitarianism is the virtue of the citizen which combines, just as Aristotle said, more than one ingredient, but always including attachment to the common good and the autonomy of reason.[48]

We might say perhaps that, in a perverse way, totalitarianism and utilitarianism each took a fraction of civic virtue and made it exclusive. Total devotion to the 'common good', the total immersion in it of all individuality, to the exclusion of everything else, is the hallmark of characters best suited to carry the message and burden of totalitarianism.[49] It is no accident that the greatest philosopher of the 'common interest' preferred to call it 'the general will'. That history did not vindicate Rousseau by making it passable to fuse that conception of the will with republican virtue is a story well known and it cannot be pursued further.[50] What Rousseau intended to be the fulfillment of the classical idea of politics succeeded in becoming but a plank in the ideology of one branch of modern antipolitics.[51] Utilitarianism, the other branch growing out of the Hobbesian root, expressed and, by the mechanism of feedback, promoted the selfishness which is now devouring, with alarming ease, the life forces of modern democratic societies. Pleasure or satisfaction as the sole ends sanctioned by 'reason' cannot accommodate, any more than other fanatic single-virtue systems, that pluralism of virtue that Aristotle taught to be the fundamentum of politics.

We live in an age in which global needs prescribe, as it were, global political answers, but the choices we perceive as presented to us by our circumstances are but kinds of antipolitics, ranging from the varieties of oppression to assortments of self-seeking. This situation is not being improved by the universal availability of telecommunications with their ubiquitous technical constraints. If politics, in the true sense, requires discussion then the necessity to squeeze all ideas into manageable sound bites augurs badly for its future. Telepolitics, if that is what the future holds for us, is just another variety of antipolitics, and again there is nothing in Hobbes's doctrine of public teaching to delegitimate it.

It was Thomas Hobbes who promoted, in one magnificent philosophical package, absolute rulership and obedience, protection and self-interest and, perhaps most importantly, the modern rationale for restrictive regulation of public discussion together with notions of public teaching by the state. He is truly the father of modern antipolitics.

Notes

1.   Thomas Hobbes, *Leviathan*, ed. R. Tuck (Cambridge, 1991).
2.   Hobbes, op. cit., p. 461.
3.   L. Strauss, *The Political Philosophy of Hobbes: Its Basis and Its Genesis*, trans. E. M. Sinclair (Chicago and London, 1963).

4. Ibid., p. 141.

5. Ibid.

6. Ibid., p. 149.

7. As he said in one place, 'gesunder Menschenverstand' is 'die Denkweise einer Zeit, in der alle Vorurteile dieser Zeit enthalten sind.' G. W. F. Hegel, *Werke* (Jubiläumsausgabe), vol. 18, p. 30.

8. Present-day interest in Hobbes began during the Cold War and it is largely to be explained by the fact that he is a philosopher of security and not of noble ideas waiting to be realized. Indeed, had the West pursued the latter project it would have had to go war in order to liberate the 'captive nations' but that, of course, would have been highly unsafe.

9. Hobbes, op. cit., p. 462.

10. Ibid., p. 469.

11. Ibid., p. 470.

12. Ibid.

13. Ibid., p. 471.

14. Ibid.

15. Ibid., p. 472.

16. St Thomas Aquinas, *On the Governance of the Rulers* (*De Regimine Principum*), trans. G. B. Phelan (Toronto, 1935), p. 15.

17. Ibid., p. 49.

18. Ibid., p. 48. This cautious attitude is shared by John Calvin. See his *A Compend of the Institutes of the Christian Religion*, ed. H. Th. Kerr (Philadelphia, 1939), pp. 212–14.

19. English edition by H. J. Laski (London, 1924). The book, a response to the St Bartholomew's Day Massacre of 1572, was originally published in 1580 or 1579; see J. Plamenatz, *Man and Society* (London, 1963), vol. 1, p. 163.

20. See J. H. M. Salmon, *The French Religious Wars in English Political Thought* (Oxford, 1959). For a brief, and since the collapse of communism a somewhat dated, history of tyranny, see M. Latey, *Tyranny: A study in the Abuse of Power* (London, 1969).

21. See Ch. Hill, *The Century of Revolution 1603–1714* (Wokingham, 1961), pp. 149 ff.

22. Hobbes, op. cit., p. 230.

23. The historical background of all this is truly fascinating. Let me just quote, as a taster, a few sentences from the *Splendid Speech in the Star Chamber* delivered in 1616 by James I, that great expositor of the doctrine of absolutism. '[I]f there fall out a question that concerns my prerogative or mystery of the state, deal not with it, till you consult with the King or his Council or both.... As for the absolute Prerogative of the Crown, that is no subject for the tongue of a lawyer, nor is it lawful to be disputed.' C. H. McIlwain (ed.), *The Political Works of James I* (Cambridge, Mass., 1918), pp. 332–3.

24. Hobbes, op. cit., pp. 233–6.

25. For Hobbes's conception of political philosophy *qua* public instruction, see the seminal work of David Johnston, *The Rhetoric of Leviathan: Thomas Hobbes and the Politics of Cultural Transformation* (Princeton,

1986). That instructions are not theorems was not new with Hobbes and the distinction was well understood in his time. Cf., for example, Spinoza's letter (XXXII) to Blyenbergh, 'Hence I am persuaded that all matters, which God revealed to the prophets as necessary to salvation, are set down in the form of laws.' *The Chief Works of Benedict de Spinoza*, trans. and ed. R. H. M. Elwes (New York, 1951), vol. II, p. 334.

26. Hobbes, op. cit., p. 458.

27. See Johnston, passim.

28. Hobbes, op. cit., p. 153. There are further references in *Leviathan* to this reciprocity.

29. C. Schmitt, *Der Leviathan in der Staatslehre des Thomas Hobbes: Sinn und Fehlschlag eines politischen Symbols* (Hamburg, 1938).

30. I have discussed all this in much detail in *From Absolutism to Totalitarianism: Carl Schmitt on Thomas Hobbes* (Durango: Hollowbrook, 1994).

31. Hobbes, op. cit., p. 100.

32. For the benefit of a younger generation who may, happily, not be familiar with this mythical figure, let me record the story. Lenin is supposed to have said that politics should be so simple that even his cook should be able to understand all of it. This sum total of politics is the notion that socialism must be realized. All the rest is but jobs for engineers. Antipolitics in the shell of a very small nut.

33. C. Schmitt, *The Crisis of Parliamentary Democracy*, trans. E. Kennedy (Cambridge, Mass. and London, 1988; originally published in 1923).

34. All that is said in Chapter 30 of *Leviathan* is in the nature of advice to the Sovereign, how best he could attain that one virtue. The whole chapter is Hobbes's *speculum principum* and it explicitly does *not* teach that an effective ruler who does not abide by his advice is thereby delegitimated.

35. *Politeia*, 1277b, pp. 14–15.

36. He who raises doubts or denies what needs to be accepted is called *kofer*. On the two kinds of *kofer* see my article 'Atheism' in A. A. Cohen and P. Mendes-Flohr (eds), *Contemporary Jewish Religious Thought* (New York, 1986), pp. 23–2.

37. *Nicomachean Ethics*, 1094a, p. 20–1094b, p. 10.

38. Ibid., 1097a, p. 30–1097b, p. 6.

39. I remember George Lukács being asked in the context of a discussion on Tolstoy's *Anna Karenina*, what are we to think of human unhappiness under socialism. He answered that there will be no unhappiness there. But what about a child being run over by a car in socialism, what about the sorrow and the misery of his parents? insisted the questioner. In a well-ordered socialist society, replied the great Marxist sage, cars will not run over children.

40. For the classic typology of this, see Ernst Topitsch, *Vom Ursprung und Ende der Metaphysik: Eine Studie zur Weltanschauungskritik* (Vienna, 1958).

41. See my youthful 'History without Tragedy', *Hibbert Journal*, vol. 60 (1962), pp. 220–9.

42. *Politeia*, 1134b, p. 1.
43. Hobbes, op. cit., p. 147.
44. Here belong the subjects of military service and its dangers of life and limb, conduct during captivity and occupation, and so on. The literature on these matters is substantial and cannot be gone into here.
45. See Strauss, op. cit., chap. 4.
46. It is not accidental that Joseph Raz, an eminent contemporary philosopher of liberalism, finds himself constrained to sanction some measure of paternalism. See his *The Morality of Freedom* (Oxford, 1986), p. 422.
47. J. N. Figgis, *The Divine Right of Kings* (New York, 1965; originally published in 1896), pp. 265–6.
48. See note 37 above.
49. H. Arendt, *The Origins of Totalitarianism* (New York, 1958), p. 207 ff.
50. See J. L. Talmon, *The Origins of Totalitarian Democracy* (London, 1966).
51. Beyond the 'classic' fruits of this branch, Nazism, communism and fascism, I would count here some current versions of 'political correctness'. See D. d'Souza, *Illiberal Education: The Politics of Race and Sex on Campus* (New York, etc., 1991).

In Memoriam

Gershon Weiler was born in Sopron, Hungary, in 1926. He lived in his home country until the Second World War, which he was forced to spend in a labor camp. He later migrated to Israel, where he died of cancer in 1994.

Gershon was educated at Hebrew University, Jerusalem, and Oxford University, where he studied under Gilbert Ryle. He spent many years teaching in English-speaking countries before returning to Israel. In Jerusalem he studied phenomenology, and his master's thesis was in line with this philosophy. Though ashamed of this fact, he never tried to conceal it.

Professor Weiler the political philosopher produced many scholarly papers, articles and books, mainly in the fields of analytic philosophy and political theology. He abandoned the basic doctrines of the former when it was still very unpopular to do so, but remained true to its tradition of clear thinking and bold exposition. His political philosophy was liberal conservative and liberal nationalist, which made him unpopular with representatives of almost every political camp. His career was sabotaged in both Jerusalem and Tel-Aviv by academics who found loyalty to factions more important than truthfulness and intellectual courage. However he took this with grace and deemed himself lucky, as he was at peace with himself. Only after his death did it become clear how greatly admired he was in many circles, both at home and abroad, and how deeply he had been engaged in extracurricular activities such as adult education and national politics, and in helping others as well.

Gershon was a deeply honest and loyal man, and he was fair to the point of investing extraordinary efforts in the study of Judaism and Israeli law, despite being a harsh critic of religious imposture and Israeli theocracy. He grieved personally, and daily, over the loss and the shame that was the Holocaust. Yet he was excellent company, always a cheerful and engaging raconteur and full of sympathy and understanding.

One key idea Gershon Weiler will be remembered for was his strong conviction that Israel cannot survive as the theocracy it is now, but must evolve into a modern, liberal–democratic nation state, even if this goal cannot be achieved overnight.

Joseph Agassi

4 Our Own Invisible Hand: Antipolitics as an American Given
Erwin A. Jaffe

SOME INTRODUCTORY THOUGHTS ON POLITICS, ANTIPOLITICS AND HOBBES

If modern political thought begins with Thomas Hobbes, the most unequivocally propolitical of political philosophers, then the search for modern antipolitics might also begin with his work. 'Propolitical' here refers to Hobbes's assessment of political life and his account of its origins, both of which are driven, I believe, by the conviction that politics is the *sine qua non* of human survival, indeed of humanness as such.

Using a technique reminiscent of Euclidean geometry's assumptions (points without dimensions, lines without width, 'perfect' triangles and rectangles), Hobbes postulates conceptual (hypothetical) humans free of historical or socially induced behavior patterns. One need not guess that this is his intent; he speaks clearly about his method. In *De Corpore* he declares that knowledge begins with 'reason', which hews off what is superfluous, that is, eliminates what initially meets the eye, to uncover a reality free of contingent or accidental elements.[1] Specifically addressing human relations, Hobbes writes in *De Cive* that 'to make a more curious search into the rights of states and duties of subjects it is necessary, I say, ... that they be so considered as if they were dissolved'.[2] Set aside what is immediately observable in ongoing political relations; conceive instead of a world peopled by humans unfettered by rules, political institutions or ethics. Again, in the most famous of all his chapters, Leviathan's thirteenth ('On the natural condition of mankind'), Hobbes dissolves or sets aside 'the arts grounded upon words, and especially the skill of proceeding upon general, and infallible rules called science' to consider humans as if they neither spoke nor reasoned.[3] By so doing, he believes himself free to proceed on the basis of propositions about humanity that are wholly hypothetical constructs and to treat those propositions the same way Euclid handled geometric theorems.

This exercise is not mere whimsy. 'The utility of moral and civil philosophy', Hobbes writes, 'is to be estimated not so much by the commodities we have by knowing these sciences, as by the calamities we received from not knowing them'.[4] By positing the absence of reason, we discover its capacity to lift us above the merely natural. Imagining a world devoid of ethics or politics equips us to understand their benefits: subtract or eliminate them and we make palpable a human world populated with desiring, appetitive, insatiable humans in pursuit of objects of desire in short supply, thereby driven inexorably into sustained warfare, each against every other. Reinsert speech and reason and the possibility and value of covenant, order and peace become manifest.

Method and message come together in *Leviathan*, where Hobbes equates the absence of polity or commonwealth with a logically conceived but hypothetical 'natural condition of mankind', a prepolitical existence savaged by 'such a war as is of every man, against every man', in which

> there is no place for industry, ... no culture of the earth, no navigation...; no commodious building; ... no knowledge of the face of the earth; no account of time; no arts, no letters; no society; and which is worst of all, continual fear, and danger of death; and the life of man, solitary, poor, nasty, brutish, and short.[5]

To escape 'mere nature', the bringer of war, humans create the polity, an artifice that makes peace possible.[6]

His advocacy of politics is both thoroughgoing and original.[7] 'Natural' humans are particles at liberty to do as they please, possessors therefore of unrestrained rights they can and will choose to give up, but only if everyone agrees to do the same. This simultaneous, mutual renunciation gives birth to a Sovereign whose mandate to establish and maintain order is sanctified by the irrevocable surrender to it of all individual power.[8] Thus humans imitate 'The Creation': God created the universe and man; men create Leviathan. The resemblance, however, masks a crucial difference: God can destroy what He makes; but sovereignty, created collectively by humans, can be rescinded only as it had been initiated, by unanimous consent. The Sovereign cannot terminate himself because he is a product of, not a party to, the agreement.

Hobbes extends the same logic into the future: The 'seat of power' is immortal, unlike its human occupants. But the mortals who created the Sovereign are no longer alive. Their silence recalls Hobbes's hypothetical past, 'the natural condition', peopled with isolated, speechless, antisocial, nonpolitical beings; and the future mirrors that past: no person survives to speak for these creators. True, the Sovereign still exists. However he was their creation, not their partner, and Hobbes's view of the relationship between creators and what they create is clear: God, the master craftsman, may destroy what he has created, but His creations may not choose to self-destruct – the God-given right to life is sacrosanct, the one right that cannot be surrendered. Analogously, humans craft watches and commonwealths, but these 'machines' cannot disassemble themselves. The Sovereign, a humanly constructed ruling machine, cannot undo what his creators might undo were they still alive. Moreover the Sovereign's current subjects are not free to abrogate the covenant that permanently stripped both its originators and their successors of all rights save that to life itself.

Politics in Hobbes's philosophy is cut loose from its traditional moorings and transformed from a natural phenomenon into a willed, created, humanly engineered entity linked to the very survival of the species. Without the initiation of political life, meaningful human life is not possible. Accordingly he regards religious and economic groups then seeking relief from political interference as 'lesser commonwealths in the bowels of a greater, like worms in the entrails of a natural man' – they are among the original modern manifestations of attempts to limit the power of government, for him sources of what, since they contest or seek to override the exclusive authority of the Sovereign, might be called 'antipolitics'.[9] To counteract them, he affirms the polity's primal authority as maker and arbiter of law and guarantor of security, insisting that civility is a humanly fabricated rather than natural response to the savagery of precivil men.[10] He also downplays discussion of the commonwealth's best form: given the demands of these 'lesser commonwealths', what is at stake is the survival, not the mere format, of a command system that guarantees peace and order. At the very moment civilization-altering changes in Europe and world-altering European inter-ventions in the New World are taking place, Hobbes portrays politics logically as the sole foundation of human civility and civilization. His political theory, therefore, is an elaborate gloss on the initiation of commonwealth and is quintessentially propolitical in that single, though critical, sense.

Surely this advocacy should have freed Hobbes's work of an-tipolitics – but it does not. The antipodal stages or conditions he portrays – precivil and civil, precontractual and contrac-tual, natural and 'artificed' – lead to comparisons and prefer-ences: does a humanly constructed commonwealth improve upon 'nature'? He says it does, but few who follow agree; they attempt to limit government by naturalizing all rights, and, as the excesses of unchecked sovereignty become increasingly manifest, as new economic orders seek release from sovereign interventions, and as representation and democracy gain advocates, limitations on political power seem logical. Furthermore, if polities are human rather than natural con-structs, as Hobbes maintains, they are error-prone. 'Nature itself cannot err', he tells us, but humans can and do.[11]

Thus an anomaly: at the very moment social and economic fluidity weakens the polity's claim to authority, Hobbes insists on its exclusive title to command. As a result and not surpris-ingly, as society changes Hobbes's political theory is shelved in favor of those that – in a manner consistent with events – justify limited government and a loosening up or sharing of control among diverse institutions, of which the polity is but one. Later still, political, or ostensibly political, regimes, each entailing a restructuring of society by the state – imperialism, bureaucracy, totalitarianism, the welfare state – lead to ex-cesses and, in some instances, horrors that are inevitably ascribed to politics.[12] Emphasis shifts from the primal significance of the establishment of commonwealths to efforts to restrain governments and prevent bureaucracies from threatening hard-won rights and freedoms.

Today Hobbes's passion for the polity and sovereignty seems out of date, even mystifying. Yet he points the way to an understanding of what we ought to mean when we refer to politics, and therefore to antipolitics. To respect and support political life, even if only in the abstract, requires a concession – and to this extent Hobbes is quite relevant – that the 'general interest' or the 'good of all' or the 'well-being of the community' are, if sense is to be made of them, grounded in a kind of political imperative, namely that each individual, given the presence and the inevitability of ties to others, act on occasion as if the general interest is identical with self-interest.[13]

That imperative, the source of the rules of the game which govern the political order or system, derives from the situations, whether territorial or functional, that foster political power – a phenomenon which can only exist when human beings come together and agree that the presence of others and therefore of conflict-producing behaviors and 'interests' requires rule-governed conduct. But political power is a contingent phenomenon in at least two senses: it is marked by the ever-present tension between individual concerns and a presumed general or public interest; and it constantly changes in the face of the novelties that are the normal ingredient – indeed constitute the history, the ever changing stories and patterns – of the human condition.[14]

To speak of politics – and therefore antipolitics – requires today a caution not visible in Hobbes's writings. If we are indeed driven by a political imperative that leads to initiation of a 'commonwealth' and 'politics', events have taught us that comprehension of political power requires more than acknowledgment of that imperative. The initiation of political relations is logically followed by efforts to stabilize arrangements and agreements, to build foundations and operational institutions that make and enforce rules. More or less continuous efforts to shape, bend, rearrange, carry out, make sense of and redefine the rules of the game also are inevitable, and they affect even institutions that appear to be fixed in place. The polity is subject continuously to politicking, which means that the rules of the game are constantly in flux – demands for change may reach a point that appears excessive according to already established rules. But to the extent that those and other tactics 'succeed' and generate increased and widespread 'satisfaction', the political order maintains support in the body politic, thus replicating in the present the coming together and consequent agreement to agree and disagree within operational rules that in the past initially created political power. Nonetheless 'excesses', particularly in so-called open societies, may ultimately threaten the agreement or consensus upon which continued support depends. 'Political power', in sum, is by no means simple: the games that accompany political relations are complex, often confusing webs made up by conflict and cooperation.

In the Hobbesian model, antipolitics, except for such doubts about whether the natural or artificial life is better, as were expressed by Jean-Jacques Rousseau who transformed the natural condition into an arcadian pastorale, is virtually precluded. Those who resist the Sovereign taste his sword. But later models of politics, dependent as they are on contingent political contracts and natural rights or on the reluctant granting of limited authority to civil governments, may encourage antipolitics. The term 'antipolitics', however, should not be misconstrued as a synonym for mere opposition to particular regimes or confused with electoral opposition that arises in the normal course of contemporary democratic or quasidemocratic practices, as Andreas Schedler points out.[15] Neither should emerging or new forms of democracies necessarily be labeled as antipolitical, particularly in states in which authoritarian or dictatorial rule have long prevailed or where 'delegative democracy' appears (a contemporary system described by Guillermo O'Donnell in terms of the ups and downs of intense popular support for elected, temporarily empowered leaders).[16] Antipolitics is present when politics itself is regarded with deep antagonism to the point where it is not only resented or regarded with cynicism but also seen as a contaminant of society, indeed the enemy of all other societal activity. When antipolitics flourishes, politics itself becomes the central target of opposition and is perceived in extremis as unnecessary, the potential destroyer of all that is praiseworthy in human affairs. Antipolitics in this sense inverts Hobbes's analysis: whereas he argues that politics is the precondition for civil and humane conduct, the antipolitical actor or theoretician maintains that politics is a threat to morality, enterprise and all authentically human values.

The dynamics of contemporary society and the complexities of political power create multiple opportunities for antipolitics. Doubts about the need to come together in polity may pull apart extant political unions. Questions may arise about the value or continued viability of particular frameworks or foundations, an issue that has recently plagued Canada and Eastern Europe and threatened the existence of the United States in the mid-nineteenth century. The democratic ethos may encourage escalating efforts to bend rules to the extent that some will propose that the rules of the game apply selectively to individuals or groups, in effect challenging the 'coming together' that marks the presence of the political imperative. Politicking may then evolve into the belief that each sector of societal and economic life ought to be restrained only by a contemporary version of the invisible hand allowing sector-specific rules to be framed in the absence – that is, the presumed end or death of – any general intervening authority or political imperative. The circumstances conducive to the formation of antipolitical cleavages, and the theories and acts to enhance them, are therefore as variable as are the political systems and economic developments currently operative in the world. Moreover antipolitics has lengthy roots, visible, as I have indicated, in the philosophy of the propolitical Thomas Hobbes, explicit in the work of his successors and related, in the contemporary world, both to the evolution of economic systems and to new modes of empowerment throughout the world. My purpose here, however, is not to explore its many facets or construct a typology but to examine antipolitics in a single setting, that of the American polity, which I hope to demonstrate has long been, despite its stability and success, vulnerable to antipolitics.

THE ANTIPOLITICAL GENESIS OF AMERICAN POLITICS

The West European discovery and colonization of the New World and the eventual emergence of the United States were as consequential to humanity's political life as the invention of the telescope had been to human understanding of the universe or the discovery of antibiotics would later be to the war against infectious diseases. Nonetheless Americans have always regarded political power as a potential threat to liberty. In this respect America's politics was antipolitical at birth.

Given the extensive American contribution to republicanism and mass democracy, how can this be so? The answer may
be found by looking, as Americans tend to do, through a lens
that highlights two political images. First, everyday politicking,
often encapsulated in the phrase 'it's all politics', which affects
all aspects of human relations and refers not only to the ever-
present struggle for control and advantage but also to the
probable unfairness or injustice of that struggle. And second,
in stark contrast, the stable, presumably near-perfect two-
hundred-year-old Constitution, a quasi-Platonic repository of
more or less fixed truths. The most generous insight into politics this lens permits, it seems, is that government is a necessary
evil (if men were angels, they would need no government, in
James Madison's memorable appraisal); while the crabbiest,
and most familiar to contemporary ears, portrays politics, even
when necessary, as a menace (to paraphrase President Ronald
Reagan: government is the problem, not the solution).
Government and politics, the terms are used as synonyms here,
are of limited or doubtful value except at troubled moments –
the founding, the Civil War, threats from abroad, economic
collapse, and so on. The only solace or relief available from the
sorry spectacle of politics is the glorious Constitution, a presumably eternal reminder of American politics' finest hour.

Not surprisingly, the American mindset that has evolved as
an accompaniment to these assessments de-emphasizes or constricts politics and acts as counterpoint to the often-noted
optimism of Americans. It presents a persistent manifold of
doubts, a dark, almost paranoid negativism which makes one
wonder whether the successes, the remarkable outputs of a
society that dares to talk almost recklessly of 'the pursuit of
happiness', can persist in the face of problems presumably
enlarged by the built-in incompetencies and evils of 'politics'.
This dark side of the American mindset is nurtured by a recurrent dream that conjures up images of a society spontaneously
self-governed – sector by sector – by an invisible hand, therefore all-but-free of the dangers of politics.

The Spaciousness of the New World

The availability of 'empty space', for so Americans came to
regard the New World, fostered a focus on land expropriation

and use and a conviction that society can be regularly reconstructed anew – assisted, of course, by 'nature' and human ingenuity.[17] That view was endorsed by the early colonizers, later migrants, European observers and succeeding American generations. The symbolic pilgrimage that motivated early Puritan settlers was gradually transformed: Americans were on a trip not 'to an ultimate home town in the next world' but toward a just-around-the-corner heaven on earth, a religious pilgrimage transmogrified into a materialism that borders on sacrilege.[18] 'Nature's bounty', as imagined in this tale, also fed the naturalistic biases of European writers whose ideas were formulated against the backdrop of the 'empty', untamed New World. Initially the opposite seems true, as we have seen in Hobbes. But Hobbes's successors rearrange the imagery. John Locke, influenced by America's presence, imagines a natural history in which the 'state of nature' is a developed and fully civilized condition, complete with law, self-managed law enforcement, property, servants and money. Early Americans, as they shook off the gloom of Puritanism, had come to the same conclusion: America is an echo of its metaphorical biblical predecessor, the Garden of Eden. American spaciousness, abundance and potential make the metaphor literal: Eden brought to life, a fecund land in which initially there is more than sufficient to go around and within which most individuals understand and operate in accord with natural law.

'In the beginning', writes Locke, 'all the world was America'.[19] Human society was born civil and civic, he implies, despite the absence of polity, and his thesis mirrors conditions in the then well-established colonies as well as the colonists' image of the New World. The American 'city on a hill', like Locke's state of nature, lacked only a written compact to affirm what nature had so well begun. Thus the basic American antipolitical mix: a handful of people, a new beginning, the exchange of individual energy for title to property, land enough for every family and a market system unencumbered by feudal privilege, in sum, a cornucopia, a life-sustaining, prepolitical society with no formal government and happily free of the commands of the privileged and well-placed, a storybook world for naive true believers. Americans decide accordingly that government is a by-product of the inconveniences of an already civil but prepolitical condition, a mere agent whose function is to resolve neutrally the jurisdictional disputes brought about by a growing population and diminishing supply of good, arable land.

What nature began so well, men contaminate. Political life and government exist because of 'natural' warfare, population growth or title disputes. Politics is mankind's bastard child, evidence of a fall into an inconvenient and graceless state that makes continued self-management impossible and requires the obnoxious interventions and consequent perils of 'governance'. In the Garden of Eden there was a serpent; in the self-managed society there is an unwanted, even if necessary, adjunct to the invisible hand – a government.

Eighteenth-century Americans – Thomas Jefferson, Benjamin Franklin and Joel Barlow specifically – involved though they were with governance, reiterate this tale. The young Jefferson romanticizes the Native American and 'naturalizes' the polity 'racially' by endorsing racism and the exclusion of blacks. Franklin rails against mistreatment of Native Americans but resists ethnic differences and undesirable heterogeneity in the body civil. Barlow's target appears to be the church but is politicized organization as such: America is torchbearer for a new, secular, fragmented society of energetic individuals whose commerce, industry, crafts and entrepreneurial activity replace religion-centered and other frozen institutions and the command structure or 'privileged orders' associated with them. Gordon Wood opens *The Creation of the American Republic, 1776–1787* with a reference to Joel Barlow's *Advice to the Privileged Orders in the Several States of Europe* and stresses Barlow's belief that 'habits of thinking' distinguish free from unfree human beings.[20] But Barlow's 'habits of thinking' come from the soil: a newborn's way of seeing and thinking in the Old World reflects Europe's structured, fixed, privilege-based orders. Here, in contrast, every infant is born free in an open, yet-to-be-completed society and thinks and acts accordingly. The American's head start reflects fundamental cultural and 'spatial' differences. When Barlow writes in 1792 that 'London is lost in smoke and steeped in tea', he is not simply mocking the English but also reaffirming his conviction that the American setting, unlike Europe's, produces a nature-driven yet individual understanding of rights as well as the procedures for using them.[21] 'I have seen', he writes, 'more liberty caps at one sitting of the Jacobin Club in Paris than were ever seen in all America'.[22] The libertarian setting is a given for Americans: why display symbols of affection for the liberty etched deeply into their psyches?

Jefferson provides the most enduring celebration of this perspective. 'All men are created equal', he writes in the Declaration, that is to say, equality is an outcome, the combined result of fortuitous circumstances and natural endowments.[23] In the spaciousness of America everything is possible:

> Here every one may have land to labor for himself, if he chooses; or preferring the exercise of other industry, may exact for it such compensation as not only to afford a comfortable subsistence, but wherewith to provide for a cessation of labor in his old age. Every one, by his property, or by his satisfactory situation, is interested in support of the law and order .... And such men may safely and advantageously reserve to themselves a wholesome control over their public affairs, and a degree of freedom which, in the hands of the *canaille* of the cities of Europe, would be instantly perverted to the demolition of everything public and private.[24]

Morality is likewise tied to circumstances as well as to an inherent moral sense:[25] 'before the establishment of the American States, nothing was known to history but the man of the old world, crowded within limits either small or overcharged and steeped in the vices which that situation generates'.[26] The good life, equality, productivity, indeed society itself, originate in the generosities of nature to which humans, unencumbered by the 'overcharged' institutions of feudal Europe, apply their individuated moral sense and intelligence to agriculture or other activities that offer a livelihood. Only in such a condition can the law be supported and government function properly, governing best when governing least. Political life is built upon a societal rock, not the other way around, as Hobbes had proclaimed and the Greeks suggested. Indeed ancient political ideas, despite the apparent influence of the Greeks and Romans on the colonial aristocrats, had been drastically altered and reengineered by Americans into an expansive view of social and economic possibilities. Eighteenth-century Americans reinvented political life: they converted it from a primary into a secondary or derivative institution or order resting on a foundation of self-directed, independent yeomen, merchants, and craftsmen. The 'commonwealthman' may be much talked about, but he is on his way to extinction.

Does one dare say the same of the Federalists, presumed advocates of a strong and stable central government, who struggled during the 1780s and 1790s against resisting 'country' interests, 'states righters', and 'localists', succumbing to them only with Jefferson's election in 1800? In truth even they did not place the political order at the center of life.[27] Federalists agreed with their critics that societal concerns – everyday exchange activities, be they agricultural, industrial or commercial – took precedence over any political construct and disagreed with them only over social priorities.[28] They and their eventual opponents Madison and Jefferson worried alike about political upstarts who might threaten their preeminence. Their disputes, in short, were less fundamental than they appear. Neither side trusted government: one hoped to enlist it on behalf of commercial classes they believed would otherwise stifle, the other to neutralize it so that farmers and others could get on with their affairs. Even the revolutionary preference for legislatures over executives wilted rapidly given the fear that legislators, like other politicians, would usurp what was not theirs.[29] The point is that, in the eyes of the American, there was simply too much to be done to justify a general mandate for an energetic polity. Politicians are non-producers in a society that values work and persistently imagines itself on the threshold of formerly undreamed-of developmental possibilities. Political life had been, as Gordon Wood points out, all but sheared away or detached from a society now portrayed as a collection of free particles whose activities were the source of the American dynamic and dream.[30]

This portrait is not simply of scholarly or academic concern but has had long-run, potent everyday effects. By separating social and economic activity from 'politics' – vesting the former with the 'virtues' and functions once associated with the latter – Americans reduced politics to an activity – namely politicking – that became increasingly indistinguishable from other, particularly economic, activities. Politicking and politics became equivalents in this perspective. And both were regarded as identical to other marketplace activities – bargaining, negotiating, exchanging, dealing. To the extent that this is so, and for Americans it tends to be so except when 'patriotic' occasions call for loftier attitudes, all claims respecting political life's special responsibility for the commonweal become suspect. Indeed if marketplace activities lead to the general improvement of society, as Adam Smith claimed in the eighteenth century and Frederick Hayek in our own time, and if politics replicates those activities, then the notion that political life *a priori* is rooted in the need to attend to general and common problems is undermined. At best, politics reduced to politicking – and both when conflated with marketplace exchanges – produces improvements only as a derivative or consequence of deal making. The ancient Greek notion of governance as true or non-perverted if rulership is exercised on behalf of the entire citizenry for the good of all vaporizes, to be replaced by the conviction that each individual's pursuit of his or her presumed best interest truly advances the general welfare. Political life's reason for being vanishes. What is the point of approaching issues as if there were shared interests or responsibilities – for instance the wish to have constant, easy access to an unending water supply or highways to transport goods or guarantees that education will be available to all youngsters – if such generally desirable ends can be reached by the simpler and obviously more self-satisfying pursuit by each individual of his or her own interest? If politics is no better suited than the marketplace to reach presumably 'collective' goals, then what is it good for? Is it not a mere spoiler, a danger, the problem rather than the solution? Is not antipolitics, open contempt for and hostility toward political solutions, far more sensible?

These conflations – politicking with politics, both with marketplace activities – help blur distinctions between 'the public' and 'the private'. The word 'public', even in the United States, had once spoken to the existence of shared as distinct from unshared ('private') matters but came to be equated with politics, and therefore, in the American version, politicking. 'Private' increasingly referred to social and societal activities, including the economy and marketplace, even when they involved governmental intervention and support – as they regularly did. The difference between things that might or ought to be dealt with jointly (public) and those that neither deserve joint attention nor can survive the glare of publicness or publicity (private) was thereby all but lost.[31] And 'public good' – once connected to 'republic' – was gradually redefined as the outcome of interest-group contests, a visible version of the invisible hand.[32]

These transformed meanings are fixtures in American dialogue. For example the health of American 'private enterprise' or the economy is obviously a public good. What then distinguishes 'public' from 'private'? Given American usage, the question is unanswerable, and to the extent this is so the idea of a public realm becomes increasingly elusive. If political life is no longer the guardian of the public good, if that guardianship is largely transferred to the economy, then politics is essentially tangential to economic activity, akin to horse trading. And if the public and the private are no longer separable or distinguishable, then the connection between the public good and the protection of privacy – derived from the simple logic of the human situation, namely that the integrity of each is dependent on its essential distinctiveness from the other – will also be lost. These changed meanings make the purposes of politics inexplicable because they are now seen as a natural outcome of self-interest, much as Locke saw private property in land not as a diminution from humanity's common storehouse but as a gift to fellowmen – self-interest masquerading as altruism. As a result politics, which originates in joint activity on behalf of commonly shared purposes, is replaced by an antipolitics that reduces the public good to a mere reflex of self-seeking – antipolitics masquerading as politics.

Antipolitical Individualism

Two forms of individualism currently coexist in the United States.[33] The first, a gospel of individuality that portrays each human as an isolated actor, is rooted in the New World's spaciousness, which once permitted conflicts to be resolved, if need be, by migration, thus literally disconnecting people from and weakening their sensibility toward and responsibility for one another. Disinterest in community or commonness of purpose is a natural by-product – one simply moves on.

Contemporary American culture reignites this feeling by teaching that success is a derivative of internal, individuated drives manifested externally by sheer movement. 'On the road' imagery is a metaphor for getting away, getting ahead, moving up. Fixed institutions – family, friends, schools, governments – inhibit individual effort and achievement. Hardworking individuals, the gospel maintains, seize the moment and rise to the top by resisting restraints. Humans are successful singularly, not plurally. 'No man is an island' is useful rhetoric to win support but no formula for success. Indeed the gospel of individuality is unaware of or disinterested in the plural character of politics and political power, the connectedness that social organization requires, or the relationships mandated by a market system, seeing in each only the opportunity for the 'stronger' to prevail. It is totally antipolitical and reflects the American fascination with *Lebensraum* and with a frontier that vanished only to return as a symbol for possibility. The open spaces literally shrank but were reincarnated by an imagery that substitutes wealth for settlement.

Crowding fostered a different imagery. Former slaves and newly arrived waves of immigrants flooded America. The nation was beset by what Franklin and Jefferson had feared, a tidal wave of heterogeneity – distinctive and distinguishing lingual, ethnic, religious and racial 'marks'. Each group took a turn on the lowest rung of the economic ladder – blacks forced to languish there for the longest time – and each, accordingly, was negatively stereotyped.

An ironic inversion followed, perhaps a backhanded tribute to the imaginative possibilities inherent in a heterogeneous society. Stereotyped groups, echoing bigots, boasted of their specialness, converting marks of alleged inferiority into badges of distinction. Politicking in the grand American style followed, first locally, then nationally. The doors to city hall, the governor's mansion, even the White House opened to individuals claiming mandates from these groups. An incongruous unity of the propagators and victims of prejudice was achieved: identity was redefined as group membership.

This inversion affected those who were forced or who chose to sort themselves out in groups – Germans, Jews, Italians and so on, then African Americans, Latinos and other minorities.

These mixed 'identities' – Irish American, African American, Jewish American – simultaneously threatened the older individuality and reinforced its contempt for political connectedness. To be tied to others means to be ethnically, religiously, racially or even economically bound to them, not to have chosen to consort with them on behalf of a general public good and *res publica*. Thus the newer gospel, the gospel of reified groups, operated side by side with the gospel of individuality, opposites – because each explained individual character differently – but allies.

Both encouraged politicking – individuals or groups seeking advantages from the powers that be or seeking to wrest control from them. Both redefine issues as governed by self- or group interest. Both reduce general well-being to the success stories of individuals or groups. Meanwhile the escalation in groupthink that accompanied the newer gospel reinforces the 'Who me?' that regularly greets calls for common efforts to solve problems. Together these two gospels underscore the degree to which the American political system has evolved into a free-for-all dominated by interests and elites. They contribute to an American antipolitics that imagines humans to be free-floating entities – reminiscent of Hobbes's particles – but who seek and receive favors from governments that, insofar as they seek to resolve general problems, are dismissed as parasitic. Could this fragmented union be other than antipolitical?

A Changed Meaning for Political Representation

In England the crown originally created Parliament and chose the boroughs and towns from which members were to be selected. By the early seventeenth century the boroughs represented bore little relation to population concentration: 'A handful of voters in a decayed village elected members, while thousands in busy cities elected none'.[34] A minority of the male population made up the electorate.

The American system also grew from the top: colonial charters provided for representative bodies linked to the crown, not to parliament – the colonies neither had nor were ever offered seats there. The two systems differed: in the colonies, in contrast with England, a majority of males voted;

class was less important in America; and the colonists were
sensitive to the tie between place and representation. They
were, after all, unrepresented in a parliament that now controlled English government, lived an immense distance away
from the mother country, and were divided among themselves
by disparate origins, purposes and charters. And their territory was greater in extent than England's. Americans concluded logically that representatives ought to live in proximity
to constituents. The English 'rotten borough' system and the
Burkean notion that each member of parliament virtually represented the nation were unacceptable to them. Nor did the
idea that key institutions – churches and universities for
example – were entitled to legislative seats appeal to them,
while the House of Lords typified a state of affairs Americans
came to regard as antithetical to responsible political representation – the seating of 'privileged' individuals.

In time, representative politics themselves – particularly
given the American focus on social and economic activity –
came under suspicion. All forms of rulership, after all, are
problematic when there is little taste for collective effort. And,
generally speaking, political representation is made difficult
by the obvious truth that no individual can speak for a group
of people and expect unanimous support. But whatever the
difficulties inherent in representative politics, the American
view of legislators changed rapidly after a short period of
support for legislatures and conventions. At the time of the
Revolution tyranny was symbolized by an unrepresentative
parliament and an oppressive king. Following the Revolution
executives and judges were given secondary and legislatures
primary roles, the most extreme version of which can be
found in the early Pennsylvania constitution. But soon legislators were as much feared as had been other rulers: they
could be no more safely entrusted with power than executives
and judges.[35]

Furthermore, given the federal system that was adopted,
issues regularly appear in the United States as battles between
advocates of more or less democracy, but Americans seem to
have encoded all such disputes into skepticism as to whether
politics or politicians at any level can ever be effectively
leashed.[36] Rulership is seen as a zero-sum game: power to rule
entails a loss of liberty elsewhere, or so they believe.

Representation becomes but another instance of political power that ought to be curbed other than when an 'outside' force is needed to 'step in' to subsidize, support, regulate, comfort or defend whoever is seeking redress – and even these functions generate debate.[37]

Frozen Federalism

The American Constitution ingeniously papered over differences among three or four fairly distinct political and social cultures – witness its failure to address slavery seriously; adoption of a bicameral legislature weighted to the advantage of smaller states; establishment through divided sovereignty of dual citizenship within a single polity; maintenance of the Union's and states' separate jurisdictions while temporarily deflecting collisions over fuzzy or gray areas with phrases that required future interpretation, such as 'commerce among the states' or 'necessary and proper'; and avoidance of disputes respecting future westward expansion. The Union, presumably a federation of 'sovereign' states, thereby fixed in place a localist bias which did not appeal to many of the founders. At the same time localists like Jefferson regarded the Constitution's failure to protect rights as a potential threat to 'natural' and states' rights as well as local prerogatives. The document, by straddling the sovereignty issue, did, however, in addition to establishing a long-lived national government, keep separateness alive, reinforcing the notion that political representation is place-specific.

What is astonishing at this late date, however, is the degree to which citizens and scholars alike still gaze in childlike wonder at the system established, as if its (ostensible) original and current format, its so-called union of sovereign entities that somehow retain sovereignty while surrendering or sharing it, was inspired by God. Yet events have made clear that the division of sovereignty is in many respects more imagined than real and that the states' dwindling significance is evident: the federal government conquered or annexed the territory that constitutes the majority of the present states and controlled the creation of new states; the Civil War confirmed the Union's indissolubility – and the supreme court agreed (in 1876); industrialization knows nothing of state borders;

commerce has an interstate, national and global reach; the twentieth century's social-security and 'entitlement' systems are national enterprises; and successive waves of new technologies – rail, auto and electronic 'information' highways – have obliterated state boundaries. Undaunted, Americans cling to the notion that, constitutionally speaking, theirs is – and always will be – a two-tiered array of governments, the states and the nation. What has evolved, however, is a multilayered behemoth: a huge federal government; fifty state legal and budgetary systems; internally divided cities; metropolitan regions; multistate authorities; local education boards; unions; national, statewide and local pressure groups and elites; and nationwide and global corporate entities. And that layering has created a jumble of overlapping and differentiated taxing policies, disparate health-care and delivery systems, and multiple regulatory and licensing practices so complicated as to defy coherence or sense. The result is the understandable conclusion that politics is inherently inefficient, incompetent and destructive of productivity.

Furthermore, other than during national or international crises, Americans shy away from either serious political dialogue or remedies. They do so, whether they are politicians or citizens, because that dialogue is always clothed in the technicalities and confusions of federalism with its endless jurisdictional differentiations and multiple agencies of control. To make matters more difficult for either citizenship or governance to be exercised seriously, many jurisdictions have in effect been handed over to interest groups – for example medicine to physicians and more recently insurance companies, the law to lawyers, and so on. Reluctance to engage in dialogue becomes entirely understandable, for to do so requires not simply a mastery of the complexities of the federal system but also, thanks to this deference to interests, expertise in technical fields that have been incorporated into legal and administrative codes at all governmental levels. Policy decisions again and again fall victim to technical considerations behind which stand an interest group or elite struggle and, as often as not, minimal regard for the public interest. No wonder the American antipolitical mindset, already visible in the earliest days of the Republic, reappears regularly and now appears to be peaking, taking shape as a permanent chasm

between 'the people' and 'the government', the former a naturally wholesome organism, the latter a predator. Be it in the
nineteenth-century writings of Mark Twain, the absurdist
antipolitics of social Darwinists, the commentaries of Mr
Dooley, or the current rage for privatization among opinion
leaders and, somewhat incongruously, officeholders, the
doubts are always the same. And the electorate believes what it
hears because the evidence of government failures seems
overwhelming.

Contemporary conditions reinforce citizens' skepticism.
The sense of being bound together by common problems and
a concern for the public good has further eroded under the
impact of the automobile, suburbanization, the deterioration
of inner cities, altered familial and working patterns, and a
fragmented health-care system. Neighborhood watches and
heavily armed police replace communal connectedness; states
and cities wrestle with one another for economic advantage
with the ferocity of warring tribes, reiterate their separateness,
and endorse the 'right' of interest groups and elites to pick
over government monies as buzzards pick at carcasses.
Competition, which after all may be normal among nation-
states, regularly characterizes relations among the states of the
American polity. In each a chorus squawks continuously for
reduced federal spending and calls for as well as uses federal
monies to balance state budgets – over and above the regular
programs mandated by the federal government that foster
state expenditures. No federal bill for emergency relief in one
state is safe from amendments tacking on grants to others.
The state of New Hampshire has cheerfully used medicaid
funds to balance its general budget, while the leaders who
hatch such monetary schemes constantly protest the existence
of a spendthrift national government. But New Hampshire has
not cornered the market in ambiguity and hypocrisy. Though
the states are interdependent, they regard one another as
business rivals. Consider the inaugural words of Christine
Todd Whitman, governor of New Jersey: 'Make no mistake
about it, we are in a battle for jobs with Pennsylvania, the
Carolinas and the Sun Belt every single day'.[38] What she
describes is a war that pits each state against all others 'from
sea to shining sea'.

What is one to make of this state of affairs in the midst of ceaseless talk of globalization and international trade? Or of the habit now sanctified by the media and successive presidents of regarding the nation's capital as if it were or had been occupied by enemy forces? The answer appears to be that though the question of state sovereignty deserves thorough re-examination, the American mindset, as has been true from the beginning, disdains political connectedness and still believes that self-managed, 'natural' societal practices – actually a barely disguised ideological version of the invisible hand – can resolve all problems. There is no want of patriotism or nationalism when called for, but Americans seem unaware of the possibility that the game of life is played within a framework of agreed-upon rules, political by definition, even in a market-driven society, although the rich and well-placed certainly understand the connection between their continued preeminence and a national polity that either serves or protects their interests. What persists, however, reinforced by verbiage that converts the original federal system into an icon, is an inability to develop the national political concord, and with it the dialogue, to tackle common problems at the federal level. Misunderstanding has been piled on misunderstanding in what has become a dangerous propaganda game that insists on ridiculing the possibility of undertaking effective joint action to resolve problems. The vessel used to give this propaganda a sanctity it no longer possesses is the by-now fossilized federal system adopted in 1787. The ingenious solution to the presence of thirteen sovereign states, a federation in which authority appears to be divided among jurisdictions, has therefore been partially transformed into a means for expressing contempt for politics. The irony is that the same contempt directed at the national government reverberates in the states and in local settings, where gridlock accompanies the deterioration of urban environments.

Ambiguity Respecting 'Connectedness'

Humans attempt to cope with the perplexities of a plural world – a world in which 'they are all the same, that is, human, in such a way, that nobody is ever the same as anyone else who

ever lived, lives, or will live' and in which they share turf and
therefore jointly confront problems including the presence of
other humans – by means of connectedness, acknowledgment
of significant linkages to one another distinct from familial or
tribal or 'group' ties.[39] One of the most persistent of these
linkages in human affairs is what in this chapter was earlier
called the political imperative which leads to the foundation
of modes of governance, of rules of the game which they
develop or foster. Americans, however, have always been ambivalent about the necessities entailed in political connectedness, and for a very simple reason. Their world was, as the
early settlers and Founding Fathers knew, comparatively well-
off, unencumbered by the tired institutions of Europe, open
to development, ripe for hard work and for picking, provided
they pushed aside the Native Americans.

In a time when shortages are evident and waste is visible at
every turn, however, Americans have not to any great extent
reconceived their situation. They have not found appropriate
ways to invigorate public partnerships that might shore up or
reconstitute the rules of the game that make living together
with a degree of nonviolence possible. Influences already
mentioned – the automobile and suburbanization, the weakening of neighborhood ties, the emphasis on individual
achievement, group-based 'identities', the growing clout of
pressure groups, and the inattentiveness to or disdain for the
public realm – have made Americans less attentive to the connections among them. And in some instances groups regard
themselves as either outside or above the system. This lack of
political concordance is not simply the result of agitation
among those who feel left out or mistreated or who have
learned that the rules of the game often operate to their dis-
advantage. Contempt for the law and the system also shows up
regularly among the favored and highly placed. Witness the
recent embarrassment of a number of would-be appointees to
high federal offices following disclosure of their failure to obey
the social-security law with respect to domestic employees. At
the same time, the less advantaged learn from experience that
civility on their part is rarely reciprocated. Still, they are not rebellious – unless we so interpret America's increasing violence
– perhaps because economic opportunities remain extraordinary, save for some 20 per cent of the population.

But as the ties that bind loosen, lawlessness may follow and be countered by a tide of decisions to take the law into one's own hands. A circular pattern emerges: disconnection from others, absence of agreed-upon rules of the game, resort to violence and lawlessness, and finally, as the sense of being joined together attenuates, still stronger convictions that what may well be social and political issues are little more than personal troubles. There are undoubtedly many pluses to 'individuality' and to group gains, among them the growing visibility of persons who in earlier times were 'forgotten', often society's victims. Nonetheless, as emphasis shifts away from the community's or, to use the old phrase, 'the king's peace', the individual's security moves center stage. This tendency, if indeed it grows, highlights the frailty of the system. In its place there are individuals, Hobbes's particles, now operating solo in what is supposed to be a polity. The difference is that although there is 'law', it is not functioning adequately and individuals claim the right to become enforcers of it, and thereby inadvertently negate law and order's purpose and impact. As a result the definition of criminal conduct is itself threatened, and the new incoherence or confusion is said to justify individuals acting alone rather than within the framework of agreed-upon rules.[40] A guerilla polity within the polity emerges, reacting to outbreaks of intense feelings that surface and disappear rapidly, only to return in new guises. The political and legal system is thereby threatened with replacement by individual 'judgements' that have little or nothing to do with traditions of jurisprudence. Such developments signal the potentially imminent triumph of disconnectedness and antipolitics, a possibility that cannot entirely be ruled out, even in the United States, the world's oldest constitutional republic.

THE USE OF ANTIPOLITICS: H. ROSS PEROT

Henry Ross Perot's emergence as a candidate for president in 1992, preceded by early-warning signals in the campaigns of Barry Goldwater (1964) and George Wallace (1968), illustrates growing American frustration over the current system and the ready use to which antipolitical sentiments can be put.

Party loyalty has been steadily weakening in the United States during the past half-century. Since Franklin Delano Roosevelt, Harry S. Truman and Dwight David Eisenhower the presidency has declined in prestige. Presidents are replaceable or unreelectable. Candidates for office are shaped or created by the mass media: Ronald Reagan's meteoric political career proved that life, politicking and film could be made nearly indistinguishable as he almost literally stepped off the screen into public life using television as a waystation in the fashioning of a political persona, thereby blurring the line between acting and life.

Perot is similar; if he had not existed, he could have been invented. His money and personal drive helped insinuate him into the public light. Although ideologically opaque, he was reminiscent of the Goldwater and Wallace enthusiasms, above all, of the antibureaucratic, antigovernmental strands in their respective litanies. His candidacy fed on dissatisfactions of all kinds, particularly doubts about the nation's direction and management. Therefore his support crossed old ideological boundaries. Right- and left-wingers, liberals and conservatives responded, though 'newer' minorities, women and gays, and perhaps even the religious right, were not at ease with him. His supporters responded to the portrait of a nation in need of a 'businesslike' management of its affairs: identify problems, hire experts, activate their plans. Substantive issues were reduced to plain, no-nonsense talk about the deterioration of American life, unaccompanied by particularly clear policy proposals (although, in fairness, his opposition seemed equally willing to say anything to pick up votes). The United States' problems, in Perot's version, require shoptalk: get under the car's hood, see what's wrong, and fix it.

At the same time Perot's personal business success partially shielded him from criticism aimed at his authoritarian tendencies. Instead his 'hands-on', almost despotic style, which looked like a liability to pundits, was an asset to Americans increasingly accustomed to owners and supervisors permanently out to lunch or at committee meetings. Perot claimed that he represented old-fashioned managerial horse sense, the traditional American reformist thesis that 'throwing out the rascals' and 'cleaning things up' would straighten out the country. This message had little to do with the substance of the much earlier progressives or populists but had a 'feel' similar to their notions that good scrub brushes and mops could cure the nation's ills by cleaning them up. Antipolitics in this version means getting rid of incompetents and replacing them with good managers. To sustain this argument Perot had two built-in advantages. As a rags-to-riches billionaire with little visible ideological or party baggage, he exemplifies the American conviction that business and the economy, not politics, provide whatever is worthwhile in American life. And he personifies computer technology's triumph.

Perot, in sum, appeared to be just what the doctor ordered. His personal success reinforced the conviction that anything can be accomplished if one simply gets to work on it, an echo of the earlier American confrontation with new space in the world. As a successful businessman with a penchant for what sounds like plain talk, his appearance seemed fortuitous at a time when Americans were increasingly wondering whether the sun was setting on their empire. Long-standing doubts about politics and government, reawakened by the still popular Reagan, another outsider, could be reasserted by yet another antipolitician. Indeed his can-do message and pragmatic ideological twists and turns further enhanced his image as someone free of commitments to programs, free therefore to face problems and insist that only sound business principles were necessary to make sense again of the American polity. And by ignoring his earlier connections to the government, he could maintain that he was not part of the problem. To the extent he had been involved, his activities could be portrayed entirely as a series of *pro bono* ministrations and giveaways to the body politic. Furthermore, to most Americans he was new, sounded like a straight talker, appeared unencumbered by visible connections to disconcerting one-issue movements or irrelevant old parties. And he was a patriot.

Whether or not he returns to the political wars seems relatively unimportant. Perot or someone like him is always likely, for as long as it persists, to tap the deep-seated ambivalence in the United States toward political life, the antipolitical insistence that what counts is not public but so-called private or economic energy. That the two are intimately intertwined does not faze antipolitical speechmakers and is apparently a secret well guarded by the schools and media.

SOME IMPLICATIONS OF AMERICA'S ANTIPOLITICS

Perhaps history will conclude, with Locke, that 'in the beginning all the world was America', that Americans were truly
born free, unfettered by the outmoded institutions of colonizing nations (themselves breaking away from old disputes,
restraints and regimes in order to take advantage of new sciences, technologies and possibilities) and that the old ideas
about political life brought to the New World by the colonists
were quickly swallowed up by events. Historians and social
scientists may take exception to the implication of that statement – namely that American exceptionalism, which some see
as little more than a myth, is justified – but they cannot deny
that the European colonization of the New World and the
birth of the United States produced novel and unreplicable
situations.

In what became the United States, people shed institutions
as they shed the clothes they wore as children, to use
Jefferson's imagery. They worked out a new republicanism
that reinvented government in the light of their conviction
that power and freedom were mutually exclusive. And since
their coming of age coincided with and contributed to the
age's new technologies, their energies were directed towards
'use', therefore towards entrepreneurial activities on the farm
and in commerce. Whatever worked, whatever seemed
efficient and pragmatic could be tried without consideration
of its consequences for the political order. Thus Americans
sought the best of both worlds, coupling antipolitical attitudes
or simple indifference with intermittent political action when
nothing else seemed likely to work.

Perhaps Americans believe that they have given the world a
singular political gift, namely 'proof' that society may safely
replace the polity as it was supposed to be or might be (peaceful joint occupancy of particular spaces, care of *res publica*, protection of safety and security) with a much-constricted politics
or governance, a withered-away state. But that conclusion is as
debatable as the belief that one can have one's cake and eat it
too. For despite their rhetoric, Americans are malleable respecting their own uses of the polity: they alter, revise and
change almost any practice, even as they cling to the words
and presumably the 'ideas' of the documents and court deci-

sions that supposedly froze the foundations of their political life. In truth, deeds have always been more important to them than words, with important exceptions at critical moments, and the emphasis on doing has encouraged a pragmatism that permits the expansion and contraction of political activity as the occasion required.

Although negativism about active government – a government that from the beginning was far more active, particularly in economic affairs, than is usually acknowledged – remains prominent in rhetoric, this flexibility or acceptance of inconsistency permits Americans to empower politicians even as they are cursed. This has been comparatively easy for one obvious reason: the Founders had been right all along – the colonizers had landed in a Garden of Eden and had the energy to seize the moment. The consequence is an antipolitics that refuses to entertain reexamination of the relation between political life and the sets of rules of the game – we might call them the games of rules – that help order and promote human activities. And it entails a marked contempt for political solutions as such, a contempt that makes it increasingly difficult for the political system to solve even the simplest of problems – even distributing vaccine for poor children becomes a victim of shoddy politicking in the current version of governance in the United States. Antipolitics, in sum, is not only inherent in the structure of the American polity and its ideological stance, it is also threatening to become the dominating motif in American political life.

Are these words too harsh, mere reflectors of a tradition of thought that refuses to accept an 'end of politics', 'antipolitics' or 'politics of antipolitics'? I think not. History is a school in breakdowns of and attempts to undo political life. The ancient stoics and Epicureans pursued an *ataraxia* that willed away worldly issues. Twentieth-century totalitarianism blended together public and private matters so that anything that could responsibly be called politics was to be extinguished: agreement and consent were to give way to a permanent and ubiquitous command system. Yet there is reason to fear that what may be under way in the United States and elsewhere is the virtual disappearance or actual displacement of recognizable bodies politic and a resultant chaos of the kind Hobbes was reacting to in an England torn by civil war. Contemporary antipolitical rhetoric does not ease that fear: unappealing chants of ethnic tribalism; unprovable assurances that 'the market' cures all ills; unsubstantiable assertions that the globe is now one (and cable-ready), therefore presumably no longer in need of old-fashioned governments. These only add to the suspicion that the world is in for some unhappy novelties.

Or do we finally realize that events do not follow the dictates of abstractions like 'connectedness' or 'political life'; that, as Joyce Carol Oates observed, 'so much that seems unthinkable becomes, simply, history, thus thinkable'?[41] Perhaps the triumph of antipolitics has become possible not 'simply' but because complicated turns of events brought down, at least temporarily, one repressive government after another thanks to the sheer futility of their practices and the sheer relentlessness of the human desire for freedom. The 'unthinkable' that followed – a vigorous antipolitics – is precisely what we might have expected, particularly if, as Hannah Arendt suggested, the only thing that can be expected is the unexpected. For what is predictable about humans who for decades are terrorized by despots and then suddenly and nonviolently team up to drive them from office? In other words, history, if it is not merely an unfolding of predictable patterns, is bound to be a series of surprises, at least as long as humans remain human.

If that is even remotely so, we can put aside our uneasiness and predict the occurrence someday of what now seems unlikely, a realization that the connectedness which makes human plurality bearable will produce yet another reinvention of politics and government in configurations that we, lacking Merlin's gift of seeing history unfold in reverse, can expect to be a surprise – and perhaps a happy one. Hope for or expectation of 'the unexpected' may to some seem far too little to depend upon, yet again and again it has been a factor in human history. For so it was during the eighteenth century when the United States unexpectedly emerged. So it may well be as humans continue to invent new activities that to be conducted reasonably, respectably, fairly and productively demand rules of order which apply to one and all. Which is to say, with the propolitical Hobbes, they require, in the 'highest' meaning of that venerable word, 'politics'.

Notes

1. T. Hobbes, *De Corpore* (1655), in T. Hobbes, *English Works*, ed. W. Molesworth, 2nd reprint (Aalen: Scientia, 1966), 'Author's Epistle to the Reader', vol. 1, pp. xiii–iv. All citations and references to Hobbes's work are taken from the *English Works*, hereinafter abbreviated as EW.

2. T. Hobbes, EW, vol. 2, *Philosophical Rudiments Concerning Government and Society* [De Cive] (1651), 'Author's Preface to the Reader', p. xiv.

3. T. Hobbes, EW, vol. 3, *Leviathan* (1651), p. 110 (chap. 13).

4. Hobbes, *De Corpore*, op. cit., p. 10.

5. Hobbes, *Leviathan*, op. cit., p. 113 (chap. 13).

6. 'For it can never be that war shall preserve life and peace destroy it', Hobbes, *Leviathan*, op. cit., p. 145 (chap. 15). See Norberto Bobbio's commentary – for example his observation that, according to Hobbes, 'human beings are born equal, but they must become unequal' through the organization of a commonwealth and the generation of a sovereign power. N. Bobbio, *Thomas Hobbes and the Natural Law Tradition*, trans. D. Gobetti (Chicago: University of Chicago Press, 1993), p. 72. 'Before the institution of a sovereign power, there is no people, but instead a multitude, a group of isolated individuals' – and therefore war (ibid., p. 54).

7. For a commentary regarding Hobbes's advocacy of politics, see ibid., especially pp. 93–9.

8. Hobbes intermittently abandons his logical model in chapter 13 of *Leviathan* to refer to men's actual practice, in effect portraying a 'history' or 'psychology' of their ever-present tendency to abandon the rigors of covenant and obedience in favor of self-concern. Men, he says, lock their doors at night even when the law protects them, suggesting the degree to which they suspect that not everyone at every moment accepts the rules of the game. There is a built-in tendency among humans to slide back toward 'liberty' and a consequent insecurity that matches, as a matter of history and experience, the hypothetical 'natural condition of mankind'. The 'geometrical' politics he portrays is thereby subjected to the less logical and less than fixed ups and downs of human experience. In speaking this way, Hobbes opens the door inevitably to discussion of 'better' and 'worse' conditions, since the ideal polity, on his account, would be one in which men never feel compelled to lock their doors; a 'perfect' Sovereign would be certain to punish all transgressors. See Hobbes, *Leviathan*, op. cit., pp. 110–16 (chap. 13).

9. Hobbes clearly believes that any institution, person or force – the church, the rich, the emerging market order – in position to command or compel individuals is a potential threat to 'sovereignty'. In chapter 29 of *Leviathan* he describes at length the 'infirmities' of the commonwealth, a by-product both of medieval and early bourgeois society's evolution, including the excessive independence of ecclesiastics, substitution of private for public judgement, division of

sovereign power, the emergence of an economic system allowing 'the treasure of the commonwealth ... [to be] gathered together in too much abundance in one, or a few private men', and the growth of 'the great number of corporations which are as it were many lesser commonwealths in the bowels of a greater, like worms in the entrails of a natural man' (ibid., chap. 29, pp. 308–22).

10. Hobbes rejects the naturalistic and somewhat mystical Greek conflations that wove together individuals and institutions into a tapestry of families, tribes and *polis* – distinguishable from one another in size but neither in character nor in quality. These almost seamless units had little resemblance, therefore for him no relevance, to modern society. Plato's and Aristotle's conflations are exemplified by the following: '[W]e have fairly agreed that the same kinds of parts, and the same number of parts, exist in the soul of each individual as in our city, ... that the individual is wise in the same way, and in the same part of himself, as the city ... And the part which makes the individual brave is the same as that which makes the city brave, ... and everything which makes for virtue is the same in both, ... [and] that a man is just in the same way as the city is just'. Plato, *Republic*, trans. G. M. A. Grube (Indianapolis: Hackett, 1974), Book 4, 441, c, d, e. 'Because it is the completion of associations existing by nature, every polis exists by nature, having itself the same quality as the earlier associations from which it grew'. Aristotle, *Politics*, ed. and trans. E. Barker (New York: Oxford University Press, Galaxy, 1958), 1252b. Since Hobbes's time, most major political theorists have resisted the view that the state or polity is natural. Emphasis shifted from the polity's naturalness to the naturalizing of individual rights.

11. Hobbes, *Leviathan*, op. cit., p. 25 (chap. 4).

12. Fascist, Nazi, Stalinist and Maoist regimes repressed institutions that competed for popular affections or absorbed everyday human energies, and they 'rearranged' humanity by wiping out targeted groups. Some contemporary regimes, by no means as draconian, are therefore less destructive, but they use bureaucracy to eliminate political discussion and, in other instances, have deprived populations, domestic and/or foreign, of their rights or lives.

13. E. A. Jaffe, *Healing the Body Politic: Rediscovering Political Power* (Westport, Conn: Praeger, 1993), p. 212.

14. On the inevitability of novelty and change, the importance of newcomers and the likeliness of the unexpected, see H. Arendt, *The Human Condition* (Chicago: University of Chicago Press, 1958), pp. 8–9, 177–8.

15. See A. Schedler, 'Anti-Political-Establishment Parties', *Party Politics*, vol. 2, no. 3 (1996), pp. 291–312.

16. See G. O'Donnell, 'Delegative Democracy', *Journal of Democracy*, vol. 5, no. 1 (1994), pp. 55–69.

17. T. Jefferson, *Notes on the State of Virginia*, 1st edn 1785 (New York: Harper Torchbooks, 1964) exemplifies the tendency to wonder about those who do not make full use of nature's bounty. Note, for example, Jefferson's contrast between the otherwise praiseworthy Native

Americans and his fellow colonists. 'This scene is worth a voyage across the Atlantic. Yet here, as in the neighborhood of the Natural Bridge, are people who have passed their lives within half a dozen miles, and have never been to survey these monuments of a war between rivers and mountains' (Query 4, pp. 16–17). See also his 'comparative' treatment of the size of American animals with respect to those of Europe (Query 4, pp. 37–55).

18. The phrase is from C. Covey, *The American Pilgrimage: The Roots of American History, Religion, and Culture* (New York: Collier, 1961), p. 7.

19. J. Locke, *Second Essay of Civil Government*, 1st edn 1689 (New York: Henry Regnery, Gateway Edition, 1964), section 49.

20. G. S. Wood, *The Creation of the American Republic, 1776–1787* (New York: W. W. Norton & Company, 1972); J. Barlow, *Advice to the Privileged Orders in the Several States of Europe*, 1st edn 1792 (Ithaca: Cornell University Press, 1956).

21. J. Barlow, 'The Hasty Pudding' (a poem in three cantos), quoted in C. B. Todd, *Life and Letters of Joel Barlow, L. L. D.* (New York: G. P. Putnam's Sons, 1886), p. 101.

22. Letter to Abbé (Henri) Grégoire, undated, quoted in Todd, op. cit., p. 226. The full text of the letter is reprinted in ibid., pp. 221–33.

23. Most men have these endowments, Jefferson thought, but not blacks, although later he seemed to welcome contrary evidence. See his letter to Abbé (Henri) Grégoire, 25 February 1809: 'Be assured that no person living wishes more sincerely than I do, to see a complete refutation of the doubts I have myself entertained and expressed on the grade of understanding allotted them by nature, and to find that in this respect they are on a par with ourselves. My doubts were the result of personal observation on the limited sphere of my own State, where the opportunities for the development of their genius were not favorable and those of exercising it still less so. I expressed them therefore with great hesitation; but whatever be their degree of talent it is no measure of their rights'. T. Jefferson, *Writings* (New York: Library of America, 1984), p. 1202.

24. Letter to John Adams, 28 October 1813, reprinted in A. Koch and W. Peden (eds), *The Life and Selected Writings of Thomas Jefferson* (New York: Modern Library, 1944), p. 633.

25. See Jefferson's letter to Thomas Law, 13 June 1814, in which he says that 'nature hath implanted in our breasts ... a moral instinct' whose imperfection in some men can be corrected by education, appeals to reason, to calculation and demonstration of the 'rewards' of moral conduct, and so on. Jefferson concludes that differences in moral codes are a matter of utility and that utility is differently understood in various cultures: 'Men living in different countries, under different circumstances, different habits and regimens, may have different virtues'. Thus 'circumstances' ultimately bring the moral sense into play. Reprinted in M. Peterson (ed.), *The Portable Thomas Jefferson* (New York: Penguin/Viking, 1975), pp. 540–4.

26. Letter to John Adams, 28 October 1813, in Koch and Peden, op. cit., p. 633.

27.   The Constitution, which the Federalists supported vigorously, divides
       sovereignty between the states and the Union *and* separates powers
       within the new national government. Theoretically it thereby bal-
       ances the powers of the legislature, executive and judiciary, each of
       which presumably checks the other two. Given the document's
       context – a new nation in a New World – what was the point of these
       separations and the previously unheard-of division of sovereignty?
       The answer, I believe, is that from the beginning Americans deter-
       mined that governmental power had to be restricted in as many ways
       as possible except in a single instance: when foreign interventions
       threatened any of the 'sovereigns'. What governed the new Union as
       well as the states therefore could only be a kind of invisible hand
       such as Adam Smith had earlier discussed. The rules for the market
       were to displace the traditional political rulership which colonials
       had reason to believe would regularly threaten presumably natural
       individual liberties. Americans thereby severed government from its
       long-standing connection to and authority over society, as Gordon
       Wood maintains, but simultaneously subjected it to a preoccupation
       with society's 'natural' laws. Political struggles henceforth would be
       seen as efforts by 'various groups and individuals seeking to create
       inequality out of their equality by gaining control of a government
       divested of its former identity with [and one must add, as Wood does
       not, its authoritative priority over] the society' (Wood, op. cit.,
       p. 608).
          Legislation could reconcile but not transcend different interests
       (ibid.). Indeed Americans went further. Sovereignty, which the
       Constitution apparently divides in two, is actually broken into three
       irrevocably 'independent' and potentially hostile units – the Union,
       the states and the people – a division that shows up not only in the
       Constitution's preamble but also in the ninth and tenth amendments'
       still unexplained reference to rights retained by or reserved to the
       people. In sum, central to the American notion of governance is the
       conviction that there is no general or unifying political or public
       purpose beyond the federation itself and the machinery established to
       preserve it. To have said or believed otherwise was to risk the pres-
       ence of liberty-stifling governments. The elaborate edifices and
       artifices of 'politics', having long since lost their sources in religion,
       now also surrendered their secular authority. They were now
       dependent on the evolving attitudes and contingencies of societal de-
       velopment. Despite their affections for the Union's power, there is
       little reason to believe that Federalists pined for an all-powerful polity.

28.   Not even the holdover Federalist Chief Justice John Marshall, who
       dominated constitutional interpretation into the 1830s, disputed the
       view that government was secondary, however ferocious his and
       Jefferson's disagreements. At every turn he protected society's devel-
       opment, the rights of property and contractual rights that antedated
       the founding of the Union against 'government', though he favored
       national as opposed to states' rights when the two were in conflict.

29. Jefferson anticipated this antilegislative feeling in his *Notes on the State of Virginia*: 'one hundred and seventy-three despots would surely be as oppressive as one' (op. cit., Query 13, p. 113).

30. Gordon Wood suggests that early on, politics in the United States was detached or separated from society, that societal activities were the source of the American dynamic and dream. He argues that the Federalists, who were hardly democrats or lovers of the masses, came up with the argument that 'all governmental power was something of a delegation by the people, essentially indistinguishable in character [that is, whether executive, judicial, or legislative]' (Wood, op. cit., p. 546). In so doing, Wood claims they succeeded in removing American political rhetoric from any serious contemplation of reality or ideology (ibid., p. 562). This also removed the people, he claims, from serious participation in politics. I believe they were to engage in economic and social activity, while as political participants, they were bound by what he calls a 'kinetic theory of politics' (ibid., p. 605) that atomized authority and fragmented government beyond all possibility of serious connection to the primary activities of the population.

31. On 'public' and 'private' see Arendt, op. cit., pp. 22–78. See also Berel Lang's observations concerning the public and the private in B. Lang, 'Hannah Arendt and the Politics of Evil', in H. Arendt, *Critical Essays*, eds L. P. Hinchman and S. K. Hinchman (Albany, NY: SUNY Press, 1994), pp. 41–55.

32. See Wood, op. cit., pp. 55–6, for Thomas Paine's linkage of 'the public good' and 'republic'. 'Republic', of course, derives from *res publica*, public things or affairs.

33. See Jaffe, op. cit., pp. 30–4.

34. E. S. Morgan, *Inventing the People: The Rise of Popular Sovereignty in England and America* (New York: W. W. Norton & Company, 1988), p. 146. See also pp. 28–54, 122–48, 174–262.

35. Wood, op. cit., pp. 363–71.

36. The ups and downs of American enthusiasm for state or federal governments, for and against 'the people', and for legislative priority or 'balanced government' and 'separation of powers' are wonderfully detailed by Wood (op. cit.) in the chapter entitled 'Republican Remedies', pp. 430–67. Benjamin Rush perhaps best summarized the American attitude: 'Absolute power should never be trusted to any man. It has perverted the wisest heads, and corrupted the best hearts in the world... . Whether that [sovereign] power is lodged in the hands of one or many, the danger is equally great' (ibid., p. 441; quoted by Wood from Rush's *Observations on the Government of Pennsylvania*).

37. Possibly not until Lincoln's presidency and the Civil War was a major reversal of the American disinclination to recognize the importance of a national political entity as such even conceivable, though there are many earlier examples of federal activity on behalf of development and expansion. Garry Wills, discussing the Gettysburg Address, points to what Lincoln was able to do in words (even before post-Civil-War

events confirmed the change): he 'altered the document from within, by appeal from its letter to the spirit, subtly changing the recalcitrant stuff of that legal compromise, bringing it to its own indictment'. See G. Wills, *Lincoln at Gettysburg: The Words That Remade America* (New York: Simon and Schuster, 1992), p. 38. Lincoln's appeal centered on the issue of equal rights, but a parallel alteration was necessary to address issues that emerged later, particularly those that involved a presumably unfettered right to 'do business'. Here the three branches at various times and in many ways attempted the alteration, sometimes with an appeal to the 'spirit' of the document, more often by not so subtle manipulation of its words.

38.   *New York Times*, 19 February 1994, p. B9. The governor repeatedly expressed suspicion of government. Almost every paragraph of her address confirmed the antipolitical thrust that, ironically, carries so many American leaders into office: 'Our principal problems are not the product of great economic shifts or other vast unforeseen forces. They are the creation of government, of government that puts special interests ahead of the people's interests, of government that refused to change ... New Jersey should be the engine of economic growth that leads this nation into the 21st century ... Together we will unshackle that economic engine from the restraining chains of high taxes'. This promise to 'lead the nation' precedes the clear warning that New Jersey would fight enthusiastically in the great economic battle against its 'co-sovereigns' in the Union. Thus the logic of American economics and the American antipolitician.

39.   The quotation is from Arendt, op. cit., p. 8.

40.   Recent settlements of civil suits and allegations associated with alleged criminal acts suggest that the political system is now so lowly regarded that exemptions from the law can be purchased like medieval indulgences. The ability of the rich and famous to buy their way out of trouble is not new, but the brazen establishment of huge trusts for alleged victims suggests a disregard for the rules of the game, thus adding to the antipolitical atmosphere in the United States. Even the least educated observer of these carryings-on – and television assures that everyone who owns a set and permits a 'news' program to enter the house knows of these incidents – can only conclude that the political system unevenly dispenses 'justice'. That conclusion inevitably reinforces antipolitical sentiment because it breeds still greater contempt for 'the system'.

41.   J. C. Oates, *Black Water* (New York: Penguin/Plume, 1993), p. 42.

5 The Public Void: Antipolitics in the Former Soviet Union

Charles H. Fairbanks, Jr

With today's antipolitics we are becoming dimly aware once again of the possibility that there might be human life without politics and the public world. We live in many groups or 'communities', ethnic, gender, religious, cultural, class, professional and so forth. Most of them we do not feel to be 'political'. For working purposes I will define 'politics' inexactly as the contested and changing common life of a community, connected with a modern state, that is exclusive of other such communities ('sovereign') and may be in conflict with them. By the public world I mean the array of words, symbols and habits that gives people a sense of membership in a community connected with the state.

These words are not only the names of countries and identities ('American', 'English') but abstract terms such as 'country', *patrie, Heimat, otechestvo*. The most powerful symbols of politics are those survivors of the age of enlightened despotism, the flag and the military uniform. In most human activities we feel no awareness of politics. In voting, campaigning and demonstrating against some public practice we feel politics. When our country wages war we suddenly have a powerful sense of belonging to a political community. Broadcasting and watching 'news' is a modern habit that gives a strong sense of politics, though it can also provoke a disgust with politics. The public world understood in this way is felt as separate from a 'private' world of individual and group tastes, connections and strivings. Politics, as we now feel it, presupposes the modern distinction between state and society.

Politics thus defined does not exist everywhere. Thirty miles north of the Sa'na airport the authority of the government of the Yemen Arab Republic ends and the control of the Arhab

91

tribe begins. Among these tribesmen there exist authority and conflict, but not political authority and political conflict as I would define it. Their life is structured by the 'segmentary' form of social organization described by anthropologists. Society consists of groups descended from a common ancestor within larger groups descended from an earlier ancestor, in the manner of *matryoshka* dolls.

> The tribal system, typical of segmentary structures everywhere, is a system of balanced opposition between tribes and tribal sections from the largest to the smallest divisions [nuclear families], and there cannot therefore be any single authority in a tribe. Authority is distributed at every point of the tribal structure and political leadership is limited to situations in which a tribe or a segment of its acts corporately. With a tribe this only happens in war or in dealings with an outside authority which for its own purposes recognizes the tribe as an administrative unit. There cannot, obviously, be any absolute authority vested in a single shaikh of a tribe when the fundamental principle of tribal structure is opposition between its segments, and in such segmentary systems there is no state and no government as we understand these institutions; and criminal law is absent and civil law exists only in a very rudimentary form. The shaikh's social position is unformalized and ... he must in no sense be regarded as a ruler or administrator.[1]

An old Arab proverb expresses this system more simply: 'Myself against my brother; my brother and I against my cousin; my cousin, my brother and I against the outsider.'

It is not clear that the 'political' reality is very different in more modern areas such as those controlled by narcotics chieftains in the highlands of Columbia, or by warlords in Bosnia or the Caucasus.

What we call politics came into being at a certain point in history, as its Greek etymology suggests, and it is always conceivable that it might disappear again at another point in history. The medieval knight, when he waged war against another knight, for plunder or honor, entirely within the law, did not think he was engaged in 'politics', nor did the pope when he excommunicated a holy Roman emperor for appointing bishops by himself. During the Middle Ages the

functions of the Roman Empire, or of the modern state, were
carried out by the local feudal institutions that had developed
out of kinship, land ownership and patronage on the one
hand, and by the church which was universal but not worldly
on the other. It took a struggle of a thousand years for national states to open a space for themselves between the competing charms of the local community and of universal faith.
In modern times the anarchist tradition, echoed in a less
extreme way by classical liberalism or 'libertarianism', has
tried to dispense with the state, and the Marxist tradition
looked forward to the moment when the state would wither
away.

WESTERN ANTIPOLITICS

My subject here is postcommunist politics, so I will only
mention the western form of antipolitics here, devote most of
my space to antipolitics in the former Soviet bloc, and finally
make a tentative comparison. By antipolitical movements I
understand first the movements against the old parties and
the old political ways that have arisen since the collapse
of communism: movements such as the Lombard, later
Northern, League in Italy, the movements that formed the
first post-Liberal Democratic government in Japan, the
Reform Party in Canada, the Ross Perot movement in
America, the antiforeign movements in western Europe. The
Republican sweep in the 1994 congressional and state
elections seems to draw partly on similar roots. What these
movements have in common is that they do not accept
the assumptions or conventions of ordinary politics: most
obviously the old party system, the exclusion of extreme
parties like the old MSI in Italy, the tolerance of widely known
political corruption in Japan and Italy.

There is particular dissatisfaction with political parties as
they now function. We do not yet know enough to define
these movements as 'antipolitical': they may represent a search
for a truer, more public-spirited politics as opposed to old
political rituals that avoided discussion of important issues
such as corruption and immigration in Europe, the deficit
or 'gridlock' in the United States. But these movements

suggest something antipolitical in the narrowness, relative to
the old parties, of the issues they raise; in their frequent
interest in moral ('private') issues like corruption rather than
traditionally defined 'public' issues; and in their lack of a comprehensive political program covering most issues and even a
policy position. The Northern League, for example, made its
cause the raising of the hitherto taboo issue of Italian unity
without proposing any specific confederal formula. Regardless
of their ultimate source, the fact that these movements typically culminate in protests against 'politics' adds to the public
sense of a diffuse antipolitical phenomenon, one that might
ultimately develop in several alternative directions. Those
movements that tend to attack the old political elites together
with the old ways could be loosely labeled as populist.

Some other powerful movements also should be identified
with antipolitics. These are the movements, spreading from
the United States, that press single issues, usually issues about
personal conduct, through politics: the anti-abortion movement, feminism, multiculturalism and environmentalism.
These movements either descend from the New Left of the
sixties or, in the case of the anti-abortion movement, react
against it while imitating its methods. But they differ crucially
from the New Left and from all movements of the left over the
last 200 years in *not seeking a new system or order.* They resemble
the old movements of the left (and the fascist movements) in
their moral coloration and their uncompromising (therefore
antiliberal) character, but they differ in their complete omis-
sion of a utopian social vision. To an American they resemble
much more aspects of nineteenth-century Protestant religion
such as the Temperance Movement. They seek to amend personal behavior by political action and by shaming people but
no longer seek a set of institutions that will accord with man's
nature or essence. Insofar the set of institutions or 'utopia'
used to be defined with more or less precision by an 'ideology', these movements have abandoned ideology.

POSTCOMMUNIST ANTIPOLITICS

In fact we seem to be living through the death of ideology in
the old sense, and it is coming to light earlier, and more

clearly, in the former USSR than in the West. As I wrote in
The National Interest,

> since the seventeenth century, intellectuals in Western soci-
> eties have lived in a peculiar relationship to the societies sur-
> rounding them, a relationship quite different from that of
> other cultures and periods. In the modern age intellectuals
> have tended to find their societies radically at fault in the
> light of principles that can be discovered by the mind but
> also can be adequately actualized on this earth by human
> effort. This relationship is what Lionel Trilling called the
> adversary culture. Such a relationship between the life of
> the mind and the existing social order has always presup-
> posed the existence of an alternative worldview (an 'ideol-
> ogy'), a vision of the superior social order, and a political
> movement that seeks it ...
>
> When communism finally perishes, there will be for the
> first time in about three hundred years no strong alternative
> worldview to that undergrinding the existing institutions, no
> vision of alternative political arrangements to sustain an
> adversary culture, and no strong ideologically driven move-
> ment to secure those arrangements. Our life both political
> and intellectual will proceed within an entirely new
> horizon.[2]

Of course, in areas where the Western liberal–capitalist system,
in one of its many variations, is not yet in place, the place of
the adversary culture could be filled by the ideology of democratic capitalism. This was the intent of those in the United
States who created the National Endowment for Democracy.
Under the communist regimes and in the immediate sequel to
their collapse, dissidence and then 'reform' politics were to
some extent ideological. But the repressive character of the
communist regimes and the aversion to violence of the democratic states that opposed them gave the new struggles for
freedom a very different character from those that began with
the American and French revolutions. Those struggles were
usually marked by the declaration of specific political principles, like those contained in the American Declaration of
Independence and the French Declaration of the Rights of
Man and the Citizen, principles that were to be translated into
explicit institutions and rules by constitutions and laws. This

new system was to be implemented by an armed revolution or by specific reforms such as the extension of suffrage, the adoption of free trade or of the welfare state. Whether these reforms strengthened the state or, more rarely, weakened it, they were carried out by the state. The decisive arena of social transformation seemed to be the state and the larger public world, that is, the array of words, symbols and habits that give people a sense of membership in a community connected with the state.

The dissident struggle against the communist regimes, in contrast, was dominated by the concept of civil society. As Bronislav Geremek put it,

> Its advent resulted from the realization that the state had fallen completely into the hands of the communist oligarchy, and from the conviction that society nevertheless retained the power to organize itself independently *as long as it eschewed anything overtly 'political' and stuck to 'nonpolitical politics'.*[3] [my emphasis]

Civil society is something far more amorphous than the principles, institutions and laws sought by earlier democratic struggles, and it takes the focus of effort away from the public world, from the political. Even to the extent that dissident and postcommunist politics were ideological, the element of ideology is ebbing away very rapidly as the dissidents and 'reformers' are ousted from politics or adapt themselves to alternative political views (as with Yeltsin, Kozyrev, Khasbulatov, Stankevich and others). Why is ideology so much weaker today than it was in 1917?

I would say that there are three explanations, all having to do with the peculiar nature of the communist system and the reactions to it. First, ideology was embraced, parodied and discredited by communism. As with the word 'party' and party organization, any politics that is highly ideological falls under the ban against 'neo-Bolshevism'.

Second, the most accessible form of ideological anticommunism would appeal to the 'people' as opposed to the bosses or the establishment, in the manner of the French Revolution. To do this would not only sound a Bolshevist note, but would bring to light the contradiction in the position of the 'reformers': they are members of a tiny, privileged elite, but they advocate democracy which, at least in its currently popular forms, should not permit elites to rule. Democratic ideology, and perhaps nationalist ideology as well, are deeply problematic in these societies characterized by intense contempt for, and fear of, ordinary people. Every day you hear about the imminent danger of a 'real Russian *bunt*' (lower-class revolt), which never happens, and hear Yeltsin derided as a *muzhik* (peasant).

The absence of *open* populist appeals is a distinctive feature of postcommunist antipolitics; at a time when open populism, after the Cold War, is rising in the West, it is declining in the postcommunist world. There *are* many obvious populist appeals, and figures like Tyminski (the wealthy demagogue who returned to Poland and nearly defeated Walesa for President) or Zhirinovsky trigger the class-prejudices of the elites, but their appeals are *indirect*; this is obvious in the case of anti-Semitism. Nationalism can be partly understood as a way of appealing to the rebellious *narod* (people) without raising the class issue (itself redolent of Bolshevism).

Third, as G. M. Tamás has pointed out, the dissidents, in their isolation, were compelled to *translate* their deepest feelings into terms respectable to their Western audience.[4] A movement away from Western political discourse is inevitable given the evaporation of the Western audience. After the collapse of communism there is no form of ideology that can compete with Western democratic–capitalist ideology. So a movement away from Western political discourse is inevitably a movement away from ideology.

POSTCOMMUNIST NATIONALISM[5]

There is something deeper in the distinctiveness of postcommunist politics. It will come to light if we look at postcommunist nationalism. As the Western ideological language of human rights, freedom and so on, inherited from dissident anticommunist rhetoric, fades more and more, it seems to be nationalism that increasingly provides the ideological definition of the political community. The first thought of everyone in the West is to associate postcommunist nationalism in East Central Europe and the former Soviet Union with

the nationalism we had experienced: the nationalism of the
nineteenth century, of fascism and of the newly decolonized
states. This comparison is obvious, but deeply misleading.

In the West, over a period of centuries nationalism served as
a means of building up the modern state against its competitors, the supranational religious community and the sub-
national local community dominated by the nobility. Today
nationalism makes the Russian parliament, in the summer of
1993, proclaim that Sevastopol in Ukraine is now part of
Russia, but does not enforce any effort to rebuild an army
capable of taking or holding the Crimea. The 'red–brown'
nationalist opposition to Yeltsin was stealing public property
even more voraciously than the democrats. And many of the
Russian provinces, where Westernizing reform of the
Yeltsin–Gaidar type is far weaker than in Moscow and St
Petersburg and traditional Russian nationalism seems far
stronger, are showing their Russian nationalism by with-
drawing *de facto* from the Russian state. In Georgia President
Gamsakhurdia persecuted the Ossetians and the Abkhaz in
the name of Georgian nationalism. But at the decisive
moment when the battle to hold on to Abkhazia, Georgia's
richest province, was hanging in the balance, Gamsakhurdia
apparently made a deal with the Abkhaz and the Russians to
undermine the Georgian army in the rear.[6]

In other words, as Tamás put it, *this nationalism is not
patriotism.*[7] This is a key paradox of contemporary world politics. Why is it so? Two possible reasons will be hazarded here.
First, when the ideology and 'party spirit' were openly discredited under Gorbachev, essential informal mechanisms uniting
the already weakened state structure were suddenly removed.
The result was a *disintegration of the state,*[8] most visible in the
shattering of the USSR into republics and then of some of the
republics into provinces, cities and ethnic areas, but also in
the sundering of the vertical and horizontal links within the
bureaucracies in Moscow and the provincial capitals. This
situation was revealed by the August 1991 coup, in which the
ministers did not obey Gorbachev and their subordinates did
not obey them.

The disintegration of the state was not, however, a simple
disappearance of power. Power tended to flow from the center
down to the levels at which it was based on more direct, pri-

mordial ties such as those of the ethnic group, tribe, clan or patron–client network. Stalinism had liberated such groups from traditional habits and made them a flexible instrument. Now, with the delegitimation of public politics, they tend to turn into 'mafias' or gangs. The disintegration of the state feeds on itself. As the state disintegrates it becomes ineffective and unreliable at filling people's needs; it falls into contempt.

THE VOID OF PUBLIC SPIRIT

There is a final and most momentous reason for the strange character of the new nationalism and its separation from the state: the deeper fate of public spirit in the postcommunist world.

A good point of entry into this subject is to look at armies, the *ultima ratio regum*. At the point of writing, there are nine ethnic and subethnic wars going on in the postcommunist world, from Croatia to Tajikistan. But of all the states involved, only Russia, Ukraine and Serbia have armies in the modern sense. I began to suspect this in Serb-occupied Bosnia, but I realized it in Tbilisi, Georgia, on 3 October 1993. That was also six days after the fall of Sukhumi to the Abkhaz, and what Georgians called 'the mobilization' was going on that day. Here is an excerpt from my diary:

We go to the Mkhedrioni headquarters where many people, mostly men, are gathered. Sad faces. A group of maybe 75 are listening to a man in olive drab uniform with an old, cynical, unmilitary face, who is discussing something with a vehement middle-aged woman. Afterwards others speak, exchange opinions with half-a-dozen people on the inner ring of the crowd. I ask Ghia what they were talking about. He says, 'What to do about the situation'.

This is the mobilization we know from television, and you can certainly see on the ground that these places are full of armed men, and some of them even have tanks and armored personnel carriers and so forth. But they are armies only in a medieval sense. The word *Mkhedrioni* in fact, means 'horsemen' or 'knights'. They are the personal followers of individual leaders like Kitovani, Ioseliani, Kobalia in Georgia; the Green

Berets group in Bosnia; in Srpska Krajina 'Captain Dragon', who left his profitable chain of brothels in Australia to join his people's 600-year crusade against Islam. The 'Georgian Army' could be understood in large measure as the personal following of Karkarashvili, the 28-year-old former minister of defense, who would not let it be professionalized because it might obey some later minister. When Karkarashvili resigned, a large part of the Georgian army dispersed, and the laborious effort to build a modern armed force began again.

People join those groups spontaneously and they usually quit when they feel like it. A taxi driver in Tbilisi said, 'I was at the front for three months!' To this, the obvious response was, 'Well, the war has gotten worse. Why did you leave?' He said, 'My family needed me'. These are medieval wars fought with medieval military organization: no real chain of command, no logistic system, no uniforms in most cases, in Georgia and Abkhazia. Being asked why they seldom wore uniforms, a *Mkhedrioni* fighter said simply, 'We prefer American clothes'. The formless complexity of these voluntary organizations, their complex relationships to the state and society, to decency and crime, have been perfectly captured by the Bosnian journalist Tihomir Loza:

> Some of the gangs were created and are partly controlled by the government. But there is no absolute control, and some of them have outgrown the government. Some gangs are loyal to one faction or another within the regime, while some are independent and interested only in money. In fact, there are very narrow lines between the regular police, the military forces and the private militias.
>
> The anti-official mentality which has always been present in Bosnia, especially in Sarajevo, is a partial explanation. Power, even when it is not criminal, does not circulate through usual, legal ways, but through the intricate network of private or semi-private connections. The position of minister or member of the presidency does not in itself guarantee power. Furthermore, the fact that a powerful man acts as a criminal in one field does not necessarily mean he might not be completely honest and well-intentioned in another. Many gangs and militias steal and profit on the black market, but fight bravely on the front.[9]

The institution of the spontaneous, informal military formation seems to be respected by public opinion in a number of ex-communist states. In Georgia there was a debate in the winter of 1993–4 about whether the *opolcheniye*, or people's militia, should be ended, now that more progress was being made in creating a normal army. The decision was made to maintain the *opolcheniye*. It is also striking that the leaders of militias that have become unpopular because of the crimes they commit prefer to remain militia leaders rather than gain popularity by dissolving their militias. Dzhaba Ioseliani was the most powerful politician in Georgia in the sense that he kept Shevardnadze in the presidency, but his popularity polls fluctuated in the 15–25 per cent range because the *Mkhedrioni* is so unpopular.[10] It is obvious that Ioseliani could have made a bid for the presidency, but he prefers to remain a warlord whose primary loyalty seems to be to 'his' men.

Finally, there is the revealing paradox about the popularity of military service. Almost every one of the militias fighting for ethnic groups contains numerous mercenaries or volunteers from other areas. Twelve thousand volunteers from the republics of the North Caucasus (inside the Russian Federation) alone are said to have joined the Abkhaz forces fighting the Georgians. But the armies fighting for their own nations under the direction of the state are unpopular, as is shown by the evasion of conscription and desertion from military units in many former communist states, whether they were at peace like Russia or at war like the republics of the Caucasus and the former Yugoslavia. In Azerbaijan, for example, President Aliev spoke of the 'recently slackened army call-up' and 'an increase in desertions'.[11] The entire battalions raised from certain districts 'fled ... abandoned their positions ... dispersed and fled'.[12] The explanation is partly that the Azerbaijanis were losing the war and that they were afraid. But there are also 'cases of desertions from the military units, that is, in addition to desertions from the front lines'.[13] In other words, these people did not desert out of fear but because they do not want to obey the state. As to why, Aliev suggests a reason in saying that 'I do not agree with the view that [young men] will have to fight to liberate other *rayons* [local areas]. All the Republic's citizens are equally responsi-

ble for the defense of Azerbaijan's territory, regardless of the
city or *rayon* they come from'.[14] Aliev seems to point to a
feeling in Azerbaijan that people will fight to defend their own
district but not the country as a whole; they must lack the
feeling of belonging to a larger whole, the state or nation, that
transcends the local community. Even in the Armenian
Republic, which is on the winning side and doing little
fighting, desertion is a serious problem.[15]

If the identification between these armed forces and the
nation-state is tenuous, to what are they loyal? The ease with
which many such forces have been broken in battle in the
Abkhaz, Nagorno-Karabakh and Bosnian wars suggest that
fighters' loyalty may be primarily to themselves; they have little
cohesion under stress. But to the extent that they are loyal, it
seems to be *personal* loyalty to particular warlords or *condottiere.*
It does not seem strange for a president to say of his prime
minister, 'I contacted Prime Minister Surat Guseynov and told
him that he has some *personal armed forces* in Ganja [Gence]
[emphasis added]'.[16] In fact these troops followed Guseynov,
who is from the Ganja area, against the sitting president of the
country in two coups in 1993 and 1994. Similarly the National
Guard in Georgia followed Kitovani; the *Mkhedrioni* (later the
Rescue Corps) Ioseliani; the 'Zviadist' militia in the second
Georgian civil war Zviad Gamsakhurdia and his commander
Loti ('Drunkard') Kobalia; the Bosnian militia in the Bihac
pocket Fikret Abdic; the Russian Fourteenth Army in Moldova
General Lebed, who wrote reproving public letters to
President Yeltsin. Sometimes these groups are based on
subethnic ties (the nucleus of Mkhedrioni is composed of
Svans, Ioseliani's ancestral group), regional elites (the case in
Bosnia, Azerbaijan, Tajikistan and Chechnya) or political
parties. In Serb-occupied Bosnia and Croatia, Georgia and
Azerbaijan many of the political parties or movements have
their own armed groups. The bureaucratic division of labor
that the modern state uses to do its business becomes the
source of loyalties used against the state. For example David
Zaikidze, chief of the Tbilisi police, led his men against the
parliament to protest the appointment of a new minister,
while Azerbaijani highway police picketed the presidential
palace to protest the arrest of their chief for theft.[17] All of
these loyalties can, under the new nationalism, be stronger

than the loyalty to the more distant state. From having been a positive pole of attraction for centuries, the state is becoming a negative pole that repels people.

The difficulties this social environment creates for the state and its leaders are obvious. After the rout of the Georgian army Yeltsin summoned the three Transcaucasian presidents to a summit in Moscow. As a participant in the meeting told me, Yeltsin remarked that they were in a mess and asked them if they had any way out of it. Shevardnadze said, 'If I had 200 men who were loyal to me I wouldn't be here'. President Aliev of Azerbaijan added, 'If I had an army I would take back Nagorno-Karabakh'.[18]

The great difficulty facing transitions to democracy in the former Soviet Union and East Central Europe is the lack of social cohesion that would support democratic politics, whether it supports political parties or the organizations of the state itself, such as armies. And this is another aspect of the collapse of communism and its sequel that we did not anticipate. Some of us anticipated that there would be great difficulties, but we tended to see those difficulties in some sort of authoritarian 'political culture', that is, in too much cohesion rather than too little. It ought to be the source for serious reflection that we were utterly unprepared for the emergence in the post-communist world of the most extreme form of antipolitics.

Postcommunist antipolitics is more radical than antipolitics elsewhere because it goes beyond trying to replace the present form of politics with another form of politics, and even beyond trying to reduce the importance of politics and the public world. Beginning from a situation in which the old state machinery has substantially disintegrated, we are seeing a further movement away from public life. What we are seeing is best defined as a *flight from the public world*.

The observation of armies and militias in the postcommunist world discloses a horror of organization that is not spontaneous or voluntary, of obedience that is expected or compulsory, of 'political obligation' to use the old technical term of political theory. There are many other signs of this flight from the public world, beginning with the crime and corruption that is so prominent in the postcommunist world. Crime and corruption are usually discussed as a consequence of 'wild capitalism' or something that just happens to be

taking place. To see the problem in this way is to take the distinction between criminal and licit activity in its modern
Western form for granted.

In the old Soviet system the absence of fixed jurisdictional
areas (especially between state and party bureaucracies), the
unusually wide sphere of administrative discretion, and
the lack of an independent judiciary or civil service blurred
the definition of crime.[19] It was literally impossible for officials
to perform their tasks efficiently without breaking the law. The
absence of a market system meant that many goods and services, and usually the most important, were conferred by the
favoritism of an official at one level or another, that is, by the
use of public powers for private purposes. When the legitimacy of the existing public world, the Marxist–Leninist
regime, collapsed and people fled from the public world, the
existing machinery of production and distribution became
entirely available for the fulfillment of private needs. In seeing
this as something extraordinary, we forget how recently the
taboo against private use of public office ('corruption') was
established in the West. Some two hundred years ago it was
taken for granted that public officials would enrich themselves
through their offices. Crime and corruption on the one hand,
and antipolitics on the other, are facets of the deepest reality,
the flight from the public world.

The epidemic of crime and corruption is voiceless but
powerful evidence of the flight from the public world. Other
pieces of evidence are quite explicit. For example in 1989 the
word *ojczyzna* ('fatherland'), so frequent in the regime's propaganda, suddenly disappeared from the Polish press. Marcin
Krol, who wrote speeches for the first postcommunist prime
minister, says that when he used the word it was always
deleted.[20] Such a change only makes explicit the implications
of facts such as the reluctance to put on that symbol of the
state, the military uniform.

Why is there a flight from the public world? I believe that
the most powerful cause is a reaction against the overwhelming experience of communist rule. After the communist experience, which was so disciplined, so regimented, people dread
the idea of being subjected to any kind of authority that comes
from outside them.

Under the communist regimes everything was a public matter, a political matter. If you drank vodka it was political; if you were lazy it was political. In the national republics, if you read the wrong poem from 600 years ago that was political. And the communist state underlined its claim over every part of life by repetitious rituals of false spontaneity, such as Party meetings and 'voluntary' *subbotniki* (Saturday work sessions for idealistic causes), and by intrusive exhortations in the media and elsewhere.[21] Vaclav Havel persuasively argued that the inner meaning of the ritual slogans which people under communism used was 'I am obedient'.[22] The state and the public world were experienced not only as all-encompassing and intrusive, but as highly coercive. And people came to hate that. The result was to destroy the sense of a public world that has legitimate power over people. This flight from the public world, above all from the state, is the gravest difficulty facing transitions to democracy in these areas, a difficulty that our social science was not prepared for.

THE IMPACT OF REVOLUTIONARY EXHAUSTION

To the deep damage done to public spirit and the very concept of a common good by communism is now added the damage done by a turbulent, revolutionary period.[23] Gorbachev's slogan, '*Perestroika* is a revolution', turned out to be true. Our contemporaries have typically looked to revolutions with enormous hope, forgetting the experience of some earlier revolutions. The English Revolution of the 1640s, the French Revolution, and the Russian Revolution of 1917 resembled each other in beginning with great enthusiasm, broader public participation in politics and a heady sense of freedom that permitted the raising of many new political claims by various groups. But these claims went beyond the capacity of politics, now more chaotic and unmanageable, to satisfy quickly, chilling the initial enthusiasm. The ability to raise more radical alternatives tended to empower the most fanatical and most ruthless political actors, making the competition of leaders and elites more intense and more dangerous, often to the point of civil war. When politics had become so extreme

and risky, the great mass of the population which was moder-
ate or undecided in its views and more interested in other
parts of life tended to retreat from politics, creating political
apathy just when wide support was needed to give fragile new
regimes or political institutions a chance of surviving. The
field of politics tended to be left to cynics who could adjust to
the rapid upheavals or to fanatics who, like Cromwell or
Lenin, were tactically and morally flexible.

Meanwhile the old institutions, symbols and habits lost their
legitimacy, breaching the dykes of custom that normally
channel human impulses toward pleasure, wealth, partisan-
ship and revenge. Crime and corruption grew, further increasing the disgust of ordinary people. The new revolutionary
institutions were usually too fragile and inexperienced to
control this disorder. And in any case these new institutions
had difficulty in establishing their legitimacy in an atmosphere
where anything established was freely criticized. As a result constitutions, political institutions and leaders tended to be rapidly
replaced, ending in the practical despotism of an extremist
leader, like Cromwell, Robespierre or Lenin. Whether such a
leader could endure depended on his ability to use organizational discipline and terror. But in any case such revolutions
were powerful generators of antipolitics. The above description
summarizes the views of such observers as David Hume,
G. W. F. Hegel and Hyppolite Taine on earlier revolutions.

It is to such unstable periods that we must look if we wish to
understand the incentives shaping postcommunist politicians
and voters. Consider what they have lived through. I will use
Russia as an example, but the same process has unfolded, with
different events, in many other states of the former USSR and
the Balkans. They grew up under a system in which every
utterance was closely regulated, any deviation from orthodoxy
very risky. Then, Gorbachev began *perestroika* and *glasnost*,
which suddenly allowed you to say almost anything. At first this
new freedom was used by principled men like Sakharov to
expound democratic principles. But Gorbachev's revolution
failed; the Soviet Union he wanted to reform disintegrated,
and the reformers who followed his flag were ruined. A new,
more extreme revolution began under the leadership of
Yeltsin, who used the Russian parliament against the presi-

dent. Now this revolution too seems to be failing. But meanwhile it has generated a countermovement which employs the same bitter invective against Yeltsin he employed against Gorbachev and which tried to use the Supreme Soviet against Yeltsin the same way he tried to use it against Gorbachev. In their increasingly bitter struggle each side broke the new democratic constitution and laws they had been trying to legitimate. Finally each employed force against their rivals. Yeltsin dissolved the Supreme Soviet; they impeached Yeltsin. Yeltsin came out on top, and those who followed the other flag were ruined. Those lucky enough to follow Yeltsin and to have survived the rivalries in his court were the winners; they had somehow become rich; but they still have to be anxious, observing the fate of those who followed other flags. The unpredictable, catastrophic reversals of political weather have wrecked the careers of apparently principled politicians such as Ligachev on the 'right' or Gaidar on the 'left', while turncoats such as Grachev or circus performers like Zhirinovsky have prospered. The most alarming thing is to see that the state they were fighting over seems to have been damaged, perhaps beyond repair, in the process. First the Soviet Union fell apart, now Russia is doing so too; the provinces obey the central government only on some issues, part of the time. Even in Moscow the army still seems to be deciding whether or not it will obey the president.

What lesson does this sequence of events teach an intelligent, ambitious person who is, like most of the subjects of the former Soviet Union, not particularly interested in politics? First, politics, once so closed, is now wide open. Anyone can enter politics and anyone can say anything. Indeed when there are thousands of ambitious candidates, scores of parties without members, more than a dozen coalitions of parties, you can only distinguish yourself from the ruck of candidates and parties by saying what no one else will say, by extremism and by theater. And where the state is no longer strong enough to enforce the law but can still confer favors, you can become famous and very rich. What is not clear is that you can achieve any public purpose. The arena of public life is too chaotic, your footing too slippery, your public too fickle, exhausted and disillusioned.

If revolutionary exhaustion pushes the politician to cynical politics, it makes the ordinary voter turn his (her) back on the public world altogether. It powerfully confirms already existing beliefs that politics is a remote, arcane and thoroughly filthy game. The result can be seen in several recent Russian local elections in which voter turnout dropped below the 25 per cent necessary for the legal validity of the elections.

One can now observe a generation gap between the Russians who made *perestroika* and those who grew to adulthood during it. The members of Moscow's 'gilded youth', the children of the last communist officials, have the best opportunity to rise swiftly in the postrevolutionary chaos. Some of them were interested in going onto electoral politics, but now they tell you they are 'waiting for the confusion to settle down'. In the meantime they all have a profitable business on the side or visiting jobs in the West. As for most educated people in their twenties, they are interested only in money, pleasure and the family. They find the idea of an interest in public life, much less a desire to make their lives there, simply incomprehensible. In the Caucasus and Central Asia, there is more political ambition, but it seems to be declining.

This process is better described by the great historians of revolutionary change than by our social science:

> After ten years of internecine purges, among the three thousand legislators who had sat in the sovereign assemblies, there is no one who can be confident of the respect and loyalty of a hundred Frenchmen. The social body is dissolved; for all its millions of disaggregated atoms, there does not remain even one nucleus of spontaneous cohesion and stable coordination. It is as impossible for civic France to reconstruct itself, as to build a Cathedral of Notre Dame or St. Peter's in Rome from the mud of the street and the dust of the roads.[24]

We have seen in the foregoing section that there is a distinctive postcommunist form of antipolitics which is more radical than Western antipolitics. This antipolitics seems to confirm the anarchist vision of politics and suggests that we should take another look at that aborted tradition. Evidence of this form of antipolitics can be seen in all the former communist states, but in most of East Central Europe its impact is limited by traditions of national cohesion and a strong state that will probably overcome it. In Bosnia, the Caucasus and Tajikistan we see the raw power of postcommunist antipolitics at work. In Russia and the remaining CIS states the disintegration of the state and the flight from the public world are less powerful but still in evolution. It is too early to say whether they will end where Georgia and Bosnia have ended.

UNDERSTANDING THE NEW NATIONALISM

These considerations may provide some clue about the forces pushing forward the new nationalism, the nationalism that has emerged in the wars of 'ethnic cleansing'. It is not just that a preexisting nationalism is modified in the current situation so that it provides the state with less support. One has to suspect that to some extent the new nationalism *replaces* the state and public spirit which have lost their legitimacy. The *ethnos* functions as a surrogate of the state which is withering away. It gives people an identity and preserves a link with some felt community without making demands on people. As Marcin Krol said, 'We Poles ... await a movement that will give us a feeling of community, but without in any way limiting our individual freedom'.[25] In fact, theft and crimes of revenge are central features of the wars of ethnic cleansing. What the civil law of the state denies to you the new nationalism permits and excuses.

When the secessionist war of the Abkhaz against the Georgians ended with the rout of the Georgian 'army', one could see on the coastal road a long line of trucks, piled high with the stolen goods of the inhabitants of Sukhumi, being driven north into Russia. In the Bosnian and Croatian wars, peasant envy of the apartments and possessions of city dwellers has accompanied peasant hatred of city cosmopolitanism and tolerance as a motive for plunder and ethnic cleansing.[26]

KOSOVO

Since I was nineteen years old I have never dreamed that I would live to see the withering-away of the state. But I have

been there. In Kosovo, the formerly autonomous province of
Serbia between Albania, Montenegro, Serbia proper and
Macedonia, the anarchist dream has been realized at least for
a moment.[27] Kosovo, like Bosnia, is the site of ethnic conflict
between the Albanians (90 per cent of the population) and
the Serbs, guarding their holy shrines. Since Milosevic took
away the autonomy of Kosovo years ago, a few Serb Stalinists
have occupied the government offices and, on paper, ruled
the province. But the Albanians have simply seceded from the
state without leaving its territory. They left the parliament, left
their official positions, quit their jobs in state-owned industry,
left the state's schools. They do not pay taxes to the provincial
government, nor rent or utility bills. Instead the Albanian par-
liamentarians reassembled secretly, elected their own government, assessed informal taxes on their community. Now the
Albanians obey their informal government, apparently
without coercion, live by smuggling and by remittances from
Germany, attend informal schools in houses and mosques.
They are all learning English, and very well.

All this is an astonishing effort of collective responsibility,
self-help, creativity and self-control. For all this has happened
without an armed rising, by non-violent resistance. Blood
feuds have ceased. When the anthropologist Janet Reineck did
her field work in Kosovo in the 1980s it was the helpless, stag-
nant Third World of Banfield's 'amoral familism'; there were
no volunteers, no cooperation beyond the family and clan. In
ten years, spurned by the world and in the face of brutal
repression, the Kosovars have raised Rousseau's imagined
Sparta without an army or a state, fulfilled the airy dreams of
Proudhon and Kropotkin. The Western leftist looking for a
new Nicaragua and the communitarian need look no further;
their utopia is here. Kosovo, I suspect, is what every community in the postcommunist world, every mafia and militia
inwardly craves to be. It shows that the withering-away of the
state is possible, and in some form it might be the remote
destiny of many of these communities. Still one must wonder
whether the Kosovo achievement is not a bubble that will
burst, and whether its amazing success so far does not depend
on a very unstable equilibrium of modern pacifism and
Albanian tradition, on the dynamism of the German economy,

and on Serb restraint in the face of international opinion and of NATO power.

Across a quarter of the globe, from the Adriatic to the Bering Sea, the state is withering away, faster or more slowly, from one locale to another. Simultaneously leaders like Yeltsin, Shevardnadze, Kuchma, Aliev are trying to rebuild their states. Like engineers trying to tame a river, in some places and at some times such men succeed in piling up new dikes; at other places and times everything they have done is washed away by a sudden flood. The balance between destruction and creation and the outcome are hard for us to estimate, because they are being determined by complex forces, by mysterious tides of history and, the state already being so weak in many places, by chance. It can make all the difference whether 200 men who are loyal are on a certain hill on a certain day or have vanished in the night.

COALESCENCE OF EASTERN AND WESTERN ANTIPOLITICS?

We see around us many strange new tendencies without knowing what they hold. In the former Soviet bloc, the past is being cleared away with dynamite; perhaps this fact destines the East to open up a path that the West will later follow. There are both in the East and in the West tendencies toward a kind of loss of the old content of the public world.

G. M. Tamás has noticed, for example, that the fading of the public world in dissident thinking, where it was replaced by the concept of civil society, has to be seen in the light of the difficulty of finding a secure place for public spirit within modern liberalism itself.[28] Tamás has gone on to propose that there are some similarities between Western 'multiculturalism' and the new nationalism of ethnic cleansing. Both suggest that some sort of primordial ethnicity is the most important thing, but both differ from the old nationalism in rejecting the extension of one culture over another (by conquest or assimilation). In this sense, both draw on the relativist or (using Nietzsche's vocabulary) nihilist mood of modern thought, in that there is no idea that can confer superiority on one group or create links between groups that are not 'given'. Both try to use politics to better the status of groups but neither proposes a specific political order that is best for man or for this particular group; both are, in this sense, anarchist or antipolitical.[29]

There remain differences between the antipolitical currents of the West and the postcommunist world. The latter antipolitical trends are much more radical because they appeared in a situation where the state was already disintegrating, and it is not clear that people in the West ever would or could go as far in weakening the state; our dependence on the state for social welfare is only the most obvious barrier to such an evolution. And there remain some differences in the basic mood or trend of the postcommunist and Western antipolitical movements. The most striking is the highly moral coloring of Western antipolitics, the amorality of postcommunist antipolitics. Electoral antipolitics (as opposed to the single-issue movements) in the West tends to be populist, while the postcommunist variety of antipolitics eschews open populist appeals. In Western antipolitics we do not see any more movements of intellectuals trying to lead the people conceived not in their empirical diversity but as an abstract unity, as in the phrase 'enemy of the people'. The Western multiculturalist movement pits one part of the community against the others. Postcommunist talk of civil society, similarly, means precisely the diversity of societies. Only in postcommunist nationalism does the Jacobin idea of the abstract people survive in some form.

In spite of these differences, the trend in both the West and the postcommunist world is away from the public world. When Western intellectuals talk about 'community' they mean not the nation-state (they detest nationalism) but the local or sub-political community. We have seen that postcommunist nationalism, apparently so different, means something above or below politics. The ethnic group, for the braves of ethnic cleansing, is beyond political debate and compromise; for the Western multiculturalist it has the same quality of irreducibility. I only wish to pose here the question of whether the postcommunist world, where past structures are being dismantled, may be disclosing the first signs of historic changes around the entire earth.

Notes

1. E. E. Evans-Pritchard, *The Sanusi of Cryenaica* (Oxford: Clarendon Press, 1949), p. 59.
2. 'Introduction', to Special Issue, 'The Strange Death of Soviet Communism', *The National Interest*, vol. 31 (Spring 1993), pp. 5–6.
3. B. Geremek, 'Civil Society Then and Now', *The Journal of Democracy*, vol. 3, no. 2 (April 1992), p. 3.
4. 'Socialism, Capitalism, and Modernity', *The Journal of Democracy*, vol. 3, no. 2 (Summer 1992), pp. 69–70.
5. This section draws on material presented at a conference at Michigan State University, 21–4 April 1994; to be published subsequently.
6. 'Consequences of Losing Abkhazia....', Supplement to *The Georgian Chronicle* (September 1994), p. 1; V. Russu, 'Gruzia: boi prodolzhaiut-sya, no uzhe obsuzhdaiut, kuda ubezhit Gamsakhurdiya', *Izvestia* (4 November 1993).
7. Presentation to the Washington Seminar on the Collapse of Communism, John Hopkins Foreign Policy Institute, 25 May 1993.
8. On this, see Ch. H. Fairbanks, Jr., 'After the Moscow Coup', *The Journal of Democracy*, vol. 2 (Fall 1991); the articles of P. Reddaway in the *New York Review of Books*; and P. Stravrakis, 'State Building in Post-Soviet Russia: The Chicago Boys and the Decline of Administrative Capacity', occasional paper of the Kennan Institute for Advanced Russian Studies 254 (1993).
9. 'A People with Tolerance, a City Without Laws', *Balkan War Report* (August–September 1993), p. 11.
10. See the periodic polls in the Georgian press, most accessible in *The Georgian Chronicle.*
11. 'Address to the nation', *Baku Azerbaycan Radio Teliviziyasi* (12 April 1994), in *FBIS-SOV* (14 April 1994), p. 56.
12. 'Speech to officials' (17 April 1994), in *FBIS-SOV* (21 April 1994), pp. 76–7.
13. Ibid., p. 77.
14. Ibid.
15. See, for example, 'Deserters Should Not Expect a Peaceful Future', *Golos Armenii* (5 April 1994), in *FBIS-SOV* (8 April 1994).
16. Speech by G. Aliev, *Baku Azerbaycan Radio Televiziyasi* (19.14 GMT, 14 October 1994), in *FBIS-SOV* (5 October 1994), p. 31.
17. Paris AFP dispatch in English (14.33 GMT, 31 March 1994), in *FBIS-SOV* (1 April 1994); Baku TURAN dispatch in English (16.28 GMT, 9 April 1994), in *FBIS-SOV* (11 April 1994).
18. Conversation with Jirair Libaridian, then first deputy foreign minister of Armenia (16 December 1993); confirmed indirectly by Shevardnadze, 'Speech to Supreme Council' (25 November 1993), in *FBIS-SOV* (26 November 1993), p. 72.
19. For these points see Ch. H. Fairbanks, Jr, 'Institutional Conflict and Coordination in Soviet and American Bureaucracy', *Studies in Comparative Communism*, vol. 20, no. 2 (Summer 1988), pp. 158–74.

20. Personal communication, 21 November 1994.

21. No aspects of the communist regimes seem, in retrospect, to have been so underrated by our analyses as its mobilizational activity and rhetoric. To recover this reality we might begin with the works of N. Leites, *The Operational Code of the Politburo* (New York: McGraw-Hill, 1951); *Soviet Style in Management* (New York: Crane Russak, 1985); T. Remington, *The Truth of Authority: Ideology and Communication in the Soviet Union* (Pittsburgh: University of Pittsburgh Press, 1988); and F. Thom, *Le langue de bois* (Paris: Julliard, 1987), especially pp. 114–21.

22. 'The Power of the Powerless', in J. Vladislav (ed.), *Vaclav Havel, or Living in Truth* (London: Faber and Faber, 1986), pp. 41–2.

23. In this section I draw on material used in different form in 'The Politics of Resentment', *The Journal of Democracy*, vol. 5 (Spring 1994), pp. 35–41.

24. H. Taine, *Les Origines de la France Contemporaine*, Part 2, 'Le Gouvernement Révolutionnaire' (Paris: Laffont, 'Bouquins' edition, 1986), p. 355 (book 5, chap. 10). Written in 1884.

25. 'A Communist Comeback? Poland's Longing for Paternalism', *The Journal of Democracy*, vol. 5 (January 1994), p. 90.

26. See, inter alia, T. Loza, 'Rural Nazism Comes to Sarajevo', *Ex-Yugofax*, (London) no. 11 (7 May 1992), p. 3; S. Flere, 'Explaining Ethnic Antagonism in Yugoslavia', *European Sociological Review* (Oxford), vol. 7, no. 3 (December 1991), pp. 191–2; D. Janjic, 'Civil War and Possibilities for Peace in Bosnia and Herzegovina', in J. Palau and R. Kumar (eds), *Ex-Yugoslavia: From War to Peace* (Valencia: Generalitat Valenciana Publishing Department, 1993), p. 271.

27. This section is based primarily on interviews in Kosovo (Prishtina, Pecs, Prizren) and in Belgrade, Serbia, during August 1993. For a brief introduction to the Kosovo problem, see F. Schmidt, 'Kosovo: the Time Bomb that Has Not Gone Off', *RFE/RL Research Report*, vol. 2, no. 39 (1 October 1993), and *Balkan War Report*, nos 19 and 24.

28. 'The Legacy of Dissent', *Uncaptive Minds*, vol. 7, no. 2 (Summer 1994), pp. 30–4.

29. 'Old Enemies and New: A Philosophic Postcript to Nationalism', *Studies in East European Thought* (1993), p. 117. Talk to Washington Seminar on the Collapse of Communism at the SAIS Foreign Policy Institute, 2 June 1994.

6 Deliberation and its Discontents: H. Ross Perot's Antipolitical Populism

Gwen Brown

A mood of cynicism, a pervasive feeling of powerlessness, a sense of being unable to connect with and engage in the political process in any meaningful way – these descriptions characterized the feelings of many in the American public during the 1992 presidential election campaign. In that election year, and indeed perhaps because it was an election year, those sentiments seemed to be especially apparent. For example an August 1992 *U.S. News and World Report* survey found that '80 per cent of those surveyed are dissatisfied with the country's course'.[1] That dissatisfaction may have had many root causes, for example, worry about a lagging economy, discontent with the choices for presidential office or concern that political mudslinging had replaced public debate about relevant issues.[2] Whatever the causes, it was clear from even a cursory look at polling data and only an occasional viewing of the televised nightly news or the daily print media that citizens' feelings of disenchantment, dissatisfaction and disenfranchisement were running high.

For many citizens in that election year the candidacy of H. Ross Perot seemed to be the answer, the lifeboat in a sea of powerlessness, the cure for the disease of malaise. In writing of 'the feeling of drift, the sense that we Americans are no longer in control of ourselves or the world', Garry Wills described the way many United States citizens viewed Perot: 'he has a confident can-do attitude that escapes mere grumbling. He does not think government is totally useless. It has merely broken down. He will stick his head under the hood (no

danger of grease getting on curly locks here) and save the con-
traption'. For many, as Wills noted, Perot was the savior who
would rescue and restore the country to its former greatness
and reinvigorate its citizens.[3] For others, however, Perot represented not the ultimate outsider capable of taking care, as
others before him had promised, of 'the mess in Washington',
but was rather, as Harvard government professor Harvey
Mansfield argued, 'our culture's insider, riding, not bucking,
the several trends of populism, ever more powerful, that
endanger our constitutional politics'.[4]

Perot's was an on-again, off-again candidacy; he unofficially
entered the 1992 presidential race in February and, much to
his supporters' dismay, dropped out in July, and then reen-
tered the race in early October. Garnering a surprising but
insufficient 19 per cent of the popular vote and finishing third
in the presidential election, however, seem not to have
dampened Perot's enthusiasm for and interest in things political. In June 1993 *The Washington Post's* Dan Balz summed up
Perot's activities since the election when he said, 'He hectors
President Clinton, throws darts at Congress, swallows up television time in Texas-sized gulps and jets through adoring
rallies like a candidate on a post-election victory lap. More
than a year after he appeared on the scene, Ross Perot continues to defy political gravity'.[5]

In August 1993 Perot made the rounds of the televised political news and talk programs calling President Clinton's
budget package 'hot air'[6] and weighing in heavily against
NAFTA, the North American Free Trade Agreement, while simultaneously touting his latest addition to the nation's book-
stores, *Save Your Job, Save Our Country: Why NAFTA Must Be
Stopped – Now!*, another in a series of tracts that clearly keeps
him in the public eye.[7] In November 1993 the Clinton administration, having grown weary of the pesky Perot criticizing its
position on NAFTA, gambled for high stakes by placing Perot
in the national spotlight once again. In an attempt to shore up
support for an impending vote on NAFTA, the administration
agreed to a televised debate between Vice-President Al Gore
and Perot on CNN's 'Larry King Live'. The debate was,
according to syndicated columnist David Broder, a 'food fight'
with the vice-president clearly winning the day.[8]

Along with his recurring appearances on the so-called 'free media' of news and commentary programs, Perot has occasionally appeared in paid advertising time-slots flacking for his political organization, United We Stand, asking that citizens send their names, addresses and fifteen dollars to become part of what he characterizes as a movement to restore the nation to its rightful owners, the people. His public visibility is also sustained by his occasional pronouncements of support for or denunciation of legislative proposals and political candidates.[9] His continuing presence on the national scene has led many to speculate about the damage he might inflict on each of the two major political parties should he opt to enter the 1996 presidential race.

Whatever Ross Perot's plans for the future may be, he clearly came on the national scene at a time when anti-Washington and, indeed, antipolitical sentiments in general were running high in this country. Moreover he fueled and continues to fuel those sentiments with speeches, interviews and paid advertising that excoriate public officials and a host of other Washington regulars such as lawyers and lobbyists for having, as Perot argues, embraced self-interest and forgotten the needs and interests of the people. Pervasive in Perot's language is the rhetoric of antipolitics, and his primary message is firmly embedded in populist appeals. As Sean Wilentz, Princeton University professor of history, asserts, 'it is his populism, his railing against the nation's political elites and his vaunting of the rest of us, "the owners of this country, *the people*", that binds together his disparate political messages and fires up his followers'.[10]

Among the questions that arise from a study of the Perot phenomenon are the following three. What contextual factors created a fertile environment for the highly rhetorical, neopopulist candidacy of Perot? What specific rhetorical strategies that symbolically encourage identification with and linkage to the electorate are evident in Perot's populist language? Finally, to the extent that Perot's message of antipolitics was successful, why was it so? These queries are the impetus and organizational framework for this chapter.

For several reasons these questions are particularly important in our study of the boundaries and intersections of antipolitics and politics. First, to discover (and explain) the contexts and rhetorical strategies that engender and give force to the politics of antipolitics is central to our understanding of the linkages between themselves and the public crafted by neopopulist actors. Second, to understand the rhetorical strategies used by such actors is the first step toward glimpsing the potential effects their politics may have on democracies. Finally, at the heart of these questions is the notion of the central role that language plays in political discussion. If, as Andreas Schedler states in his introduction to this volume, the distinctive medium of democratic politics (indeed of politics as such) is language, then the exploration of how one specific actor's language functions as a rhetoric of antipolitics can serve as a catalyst for future research and understanding. At the very least such an exploration will remind us, as rhetorical theorist Kenneth Burke has said, that 'we are using language, [and] it is using us'.[11]

THE 1992 PRESIDENTIAL CAMPAIGN

The mood of the electorate as it approached the 1992 presidential election was, as a Kettering Foundation Report entitled 'Citizens and Politics: A View from Main Street America' found, not one of 'apathy, but impotence'.[12] Although one may argue that the roots of this current sense of cynicism and powerlessness can be traced as far back as the fall of President Richard Nixon and the deterioration of confidence in the office, and indeed in government in general, brought on by Watergate, it must be remembered that citizens seemed quite content with the election of Ronald Reagan in 1980, his return to office in 1984, and with what many took to be a continuation of Reagan's ideological principles and governing practices in George Bush's election in 1988. In fact, one year before the 1992 elections, Bush enjoyed high approval ratings and seemed confidently on his way to a second term.

In the first few months of 1991 Bush could not only claim victory in the battle to oust Iraq from Kuwait, but also victory in garnering the highest of presidential approval ratings. One may say that such high approval ratings should not be considered unusual, given that the people tend to support and rally around a president in times of crisis. Nonetheless these ratings were extremely impressive, so impressive that reelection for President Bush seemed a certainty at that time, and some who once were counted as presidential hopefuls among the Democrats disavowed any desire to run for the office.[13] George Bush seemed unbeatable, and praise abounded for his leadership of the Gulf War allied coalition.

One year later, however, the tide had clearly turned for George Bush.[14] With the opening of primary season in January of 1992, six Democrats had entered the race and had begun to challenge the once seemingly indomitable president. Even in the ranks of the president's own party, candidate Patrick Buchanan offered up a formidable challenge in the New Hampshire primary. Facing opposition in his own party and from the various Democratic contenders during the presidential primary season, Bush saw his approval ratings drop to 39 per cent in late February.[15] By March, syndicated columnist Mark Shields heralded the end of Bush's good fortune by noting that the 'Gulf glow' had faded.[16] Unfortunately for President Bush, worse news was yet to come. By the summer, as he prepared to accept the nomination of his party, Bush surely must have realized the desperate plight he was in. In August 1992 he had plummeted from a Gulf War high approval rating of 90 per cent to an all-time low of 35 per cent.[17]

As confidence in Bush waned, citizens turned their attention to the six Democratic contenders and found little to offer hope. By the July convention of the Democratic Party, Arkansas Governor Bill Clinton, who had rebounded from a second place showing in the first primary and won victories in subsequent races, was named that party's nominee. However Clinton's strong showing in the primaries did not mean that his move toward nomination was unproblematic.[18]

As each month of the primary season passed, new charges against Bill Clinton were leveled. January brought charges of marital infidelity reminiscent of Senator Gary Hart's derailed 1988 presidential aspirations; February brought charges of avoiding military service in Vietnam; March brought charges of questionable business dealings in his home state of Arkansas and charges of marijuana use; April brought additional charges concerning the military draft. Clinton seemed perpetually plagued during the primaries and seemed to be handing the Republicans the very issues of character and trust they could use to win the fall general election.

In the midst of the primaries, no Democrat seemed to capture voters' attention and garner their undivided support, and with his presidential approval ratings in a downhill slide, George Bush, although clearly winning his party's nomination, fared little better in the eyes of voters. The result of this lack of enthusiasm for Bush was a pre-convention discussion of the possibilities of Bush stepping aside and being replaced by a candidate who might more effectively spark citizens' imaginations and their support.[19] By the close of the primary season, voters' lack of enthusiasm for the candidates had become clear. Charles Krauthammer, writing for *The Washington Post*, evoked that lack of enthusiasm when he said, 'American decline is the subtext of this election. People feel it. They fear it. And they are convinced that the two major parties and their candidates will do nothing about it'.[20] And indeed voter statistics seemed to bear out Krauthammer's conclusions. The Center for the Study of the Electorate found that none of the states that conduct primaries reported an increase in voter turnout, and many reported declines.[21]

THE TALK SHOW CANDIDATE: 'I CAN FIX IT'

A sitting president who drew little support, a Democratic challenger around whom allegations were piled high, an economy seemingly in desperate need of resuscitation, a congressional bank scandal and members of Congress tainted by charges of scandal – all were contributors to the mood of the nation, 'the feeling of drift, the sense that we Americans are no longer in control of ourselves or the world'.[22] The nation was primed for news of a different sort and, with one appearance in late February on CNN's 'Larry King Live' two days after the nation's first primary, H. Ross Perot provided that news: he would seek the office of President of the United States if supporters in all fifty states showed confidence in him by placing his name on the ballot.

With his folksy speech patterns and seemingly straightforward language, Perot presented quite a contrast to 'politics as usual'. The story of his background seemed to mirror the elusive American Dream. He began as a simple salesman, moved his family from Texarkana to the big and promising city of Dallas with all of their belongings in the back seat of the car, struck upon a novel idea from which he developed his own computer company, combined ingenuity and skill to parlay that small company into a booming enterprise and turn his meager resources into incredible wealth, and generously provided a helping hand as philanthropist to the needy. His life had already crossed from the private sector into the public: Perot gave his time and effort as a concerned citizen to his state, and provided a patriot's advice, counsel, and assistance to the elected leaders of his country.[23] As James Ceaser and Andrew Busch skillfully summarize it in their book *Upside Down and Inside Out: The 1992 Elections and American Politics*, voters' initial image of Perot was

> one-part Horatio Alger – a classic self-made man who prevailed over circumstance to create a business empire – and one-part Cincinnatus – a super patriot willing to sacrifice all for his countrymen, including pursuing the fate of America's forgotten Vietnam War POWs and MIAs. Of all of Perot's exploits, there was one that stood out for capturing his true grit: the rescue mission Perot planned and directed to save two of his employees from an Iranian jail in 1979, at the height of the Ayatollah's reign. The story of this rescue, told in the 1984 book *On Wings of Eagles* and later in a made-for-TV movie, demonstrated Perot's loyalty and his action-oriented style of patriotism. Perot showed American resolve at just the moment when the Iranian revolutionary leaders were humiliating the United States government and its President. Ross Perot's foreign policy succeeded where the United States government's had failed. Here was evidence that Perot could 'just do it', whereas the politicians could not. While they just talked, he acted. He was Nike-man.[24]

Some news media would report that Perot had made his millions as a result of his successful lobbying of powerful figures in government (mostly at the state level) to secure contracts for his computer company to write software for administering two of the nation's major welfare programs, Medicare and Medicaid.[25] Despite this little-discussed history, Perot represented himself as the consummate outsider who could talk

sense to both Congress and the people. For a nation dis-
pleased with the choices for office offered up by the traditional parties, disheartened by what seemed a lack of progress
toward social and economic reforms, and disgusted with the
scandal du jour political reports featured on the nightly news
and in the pages of the nation's newspapers, Ross Perot was a
compelling choice. Early in April *The Wall Street Journal*
dubbed Perot a formidable threat to Republicans and
Democrats;[26] by mid-April *The Wall Street Journal/NBC News Poll*
showed that while Bush would garner 38 per cent of the vote
and Clinton 30 per cent, Perot would claim 26 per cent;[27] and
by late April that same poll would report that, of those voters
indicating knowledge of Perot, 61 per cent would support him
for office.[28] And even though he officially withdrew in July
from a race of which he had never officially been a part, and
then announced his return in October, Perot still commanded
support. *The Washington Post* reported in late October that,
although Perot's strength had flagged since the spring, it was
rising again.[29]

Against the backdrop of an unpopular president, a scandal-
weakened opponent and a distrust of government, Perot's
message was plain and simple: government is in bad shape
and I'm just the outsider who can fix it. For Perot the problem
with the nation was not the nation itself, that is, the people.
Rather the problem was the lack of appropriate action on the
part of the people's government, a lack of action that was the
consequence of several causes: career politicians who had lost
touch with the problems of the average citizen; an electoral
system driven by the moneyed interests of political action com-
mittees; lobbyists who are 'fellows with thousand-dollar suits
and alligator shoes running up and down the halls of
Congress'[30] in an attempt to make policy; and a red-tape-
bound, insular and incestuous bureaucracy more concerned
about its own perpetuity and growth than about working for
and solving the problems of the people. The answer to this
problem of a lack of action, according to Perot, was a different
kind of president and a people in more direct control of their
governance.

How would Perot function as a different kind of president
and provide government that, as he was fond of saying, 'comes
from the people' and not 'at the people'? He would get the

Republicans and the Democrats to 'hold hands'[31] and work to-gether. According to Perot, '[t]here are great plans lying all over Washington [that] nobody ever executes. It's like having a blueprint for a house you never built. You don't have any-where to sleep'.[32] He would take the 'best plans' and then 'have a raging debate about those plans. Then out of that debate, with leadership comes consensus. Then, if the plans are huge and complex like health care, I would urge you to implement pilot programs ... [F]inally, our government passes laws and freezes the plan in concrete'.[33] An alternative process that Perot also persistently touted was the electronic town hall meeting in which 'we will take the facts and explain the facts in detail to the American people. And we'll say, "Here is where we are. Now you own this country, ... and we're not going to sound-bite you." ... We go to the American people on tele-vision ... and say "Here are the alternatives ... Which ... do you feel is best?" ... The ... people react, by congressional dis-trict, and we know what the people want'.[34] Exactly how Perot (or any other prospective president) would fit into this plan, however, is not particularly clear. What Perot told us, though, was that he had 'a lot of experience in getting things done'[35] and that he and the American people could change govern-ment: 'Then the question is, can we govern? I love that one. The "we" is you and me. You bet your hat we can govern because we will be in there together and we will figure out what to do'.[36]

Two dominant metaphors in Perot's rhetoric gave force to his call for a different kind of president and more direct control by the people: the metaphors of sports and war. For example Perot urged the nation to pull together because '[d]ivided teams lose; united teams win';[37] he called upon the volunteers of his organization to become an 'army of patriots' and 'draw a line in the sand';[38] he cited the need for the House, the Senate and the White House to 'march in step';[39] of the political campaign process, he argued that 'I should not be able to beat you because I destroy you ... This is mud wrestling with no rules';[40] he asked, given the choice of the three candidates, '[i]f you are going into combat, which one would you want by your side?'[41] and he often noted that 'we're really going to get down in the trenches'[42] to solve the nation's problems. By coopting the language used prominently in media, the language of sports and war,[43] Perot turned the metaphors – metaphors in which voters were well-schooled – to his favor. In the game of politics, Perot would meet the adversary and wage battle. The adversary, however, would not be the one identified in the media version of the metaphor, that is, Perot's electoral opponents; his adversary would instead be the system, the government that is 'supposed to come from the people,' but instead 'comes at the people'.[44]

In exclaiming that 'we've got to turn this thing around' and then defining the 'we' as 'you and me',[45] Perot invited the nation to become participants in the battle, not merely spectators on the sidelines. Thus, for a nation disenchanted with its elected (and potential) leaders, dissatisfied with its role in the country's course and seemingly frustrated at having its complaints and concerns unheeded, Perot, through his rhetorical 'arsenal', gave voice to many citizens' alienation and provided an electoral alternative for their votes. He would fight for the people; he would be 'the candidate that worked and belonged to nobody'; he would be the people's 'servant' and 'belong to them'.[46]

The primary channel through which Perot carried his message was television, a medium that made available to him two vehicles: the 'free' talk shows on which he appeared as a guest, and the paid 'infomercials' and advertisements he produced in his own campaign. Without television the Perot campaign might never have existed; in fact some would argue that the Perot campaign was little more than a media event with no real tie to reality, much less to constitutional democracy.[47] On the televised talk shows Perot was a success. Tom Shales wrote of his television performances that,

> [b]y accepted standards, he is not telegenic. He is awkward and odd-looking, he has a whiny voice and a heavy accent, and he comes across alternately as cold or as rantingly hostile.
>
> But the audience apparently sees 'cold' as businesslike, 'awkward' as authentic, 'hostile' as courageous, and all the other rough edges as evidence to support Perot's insistence that he is an outsider and therefore unlike all other political candidates.[48]

Both talk shows and regular news broadcasts provided voters with the visual and verbal evidence that Perot was different from his competitors, but it was the talk shows, with the opportunity they provided him to control the transmission of his message, that made 'different' into a quality clearly appealing to them.

On 3 November 1992 the nation's citizens went to the polls and cast their votes in the highest numbers since 1972.[49] Seventeen million of those voters were young people between the ages of eighteen and twenty nine, an all-time record for that age group.[50] Nineteen per cent of those who voted selected as their choice Ross Perot (though in the American electoral college scheme for choosing presidents, this translated into zero electoral votes, as he carried a plurality in no states). The reasons for the rise of and support for the third-party candidacy of Ross Perot and for his receiving the largest percentage of votes since Theodore Roosevelt are many and complex. However chief among those reasons is that Ross Perot's message resonated with the electorate in its ability to tap into the prevailing mood of the nation and in its ability to identify and articulate at a national level the concerns of many citizens about their government.

Central to Perot's relative success in the 1992 campaign was a rhetoric of neopopulism and antipolitics, a rhetoric that argued that government had become distanced from and unresponsive to citizens' concerns; that government had grown large, cumbersome, inert and incapable of anything except gridlock; that government catered to and encouraged special interests whose only interest was in procuring favor for a few; and that government had lost sight of its role as servant to the people. At the heart of Perot's relative success was his ability to give rhetorical locus to the sense of dislocation, alienation and dissatisfaction felt by many citizens. To understand more specifically the success of Perot's antipolitical, neopopulist message, though, requires an explication of the three dominant rhetorical strategies he used during the campaign.

RHETORICAL STRATEGIES

H. Ross Perot gained his prominent role in the 1992 election and has since maintained that role through the use of three dominant rhetorical strategies. First, Perot created and sustained an argument for citizens to conceive of him as fit to occupy a position of national leadership by developing a narrative which conjoins two populist myths: an inefficient and ineffectual government, and the hero/outsider capable of creating governmental change and reform. These are, of course, venerable myths with successful histories on the American political scene. Second, within that narrative structure, Perot, as the hero/outsider, employs synecdochic language strategies and enthymemetic reasoning structures to reduce complex problems to simple and solvable issues.[51] Third, through specific language choices, Perot creates the illusion that he has provided his audience with essential information, as well as the illusion that deliberation has already occurred or will occur; he then invites the audience to agree upon a movement to action. All three of these strategies work in concert to create a populist rhetoric of antipolitics. Analyzing Perot's rhetoric from the perspective of Walter Fisher's narrative paradigm can demonstrate how these three strategies function together to that end.

Fisher suggests that 'human communication should be viewed as historical as well as situational, as stories competing with other stories constituted by good reasons, as being rational when they satisfy the demands of narrative probability and narrative fidelity, and as inevitably moral inducements'.[52] Simply put, narratives or stories argue and, when they are judged by hearers to be 'coherent' and 'ring true with the stories they know to be true in their lives',[53] they argue successfully because they are understood to have provided 'good reasons'. Moreover, because stories consist of dramatic elements of plot, character, scene and motivations, they lead to an end, a conclusion, a point. For example I remember my mother often telling me as a child any number of versions of a story which always began with the words 'There once was a little girl ... ' Upon hearing the opening line I knew that what would follow would be a story in which I was expected to place myself and to learn vicariously the lesson or lessons it taught. The story produced a moral stance and moral inducement concerning good and bad, appropriate and inappropriate, or useful and harmful ways of thinking and behaving.

For Fisher the traditional perspective, what he calls the 'rational world paradigm', is insufficient as an explanation for understanding human communication. That paradigm, which suggests that we understand and make sense of our experiences as though they were 'a set of logical puzzles which can be resolved through appropriate analysis and application of reason conceived as an argumentative construct',[54] is lacking in Fisher's view in that it does not account for the process by which humans are able to agree on the meanings of symbolizations which seem not to possess a rational core. Instead Fisher argues for the 'narrative world paradigm', which he sees as subsuming the rational and which he thinks provides more explanatory richness for understanding the nature of human communication. For Fisher, then, the narrative is architectonic, more encompassing than the rational in its power to explain, and yet still compatible with the rational in its ability to borrow from it.

While I find Fisher's notions of the narrative useful and enlightening, my own view is that he has not found the completely 'elegant' paradigmatic explanation. Rather than view narrative as the overarching explanation of human communication, I see it as another form, distinct from the 'rational', one that allows us to make sense of experiences in different ways. That difference of opinion acknowledged, I believe that Fisher is correct in asserting that narrative can argue and argue powerfully. Evidence of that ability can be found in the narrative employed by Ross Perot, a narrative which brings together two familiar myths.

Bad Government

The first myth is that the government is inefficient and ineffectual in its ability to manage the nation's affairs and solve the nation's problems. This myth provided a fertile environment for the mood of discontent the nation experienced during the campaign, and Ross Perot spent his candidacy certifying that both myth and mood were accurate. His consistent assertions that the country had been 'mismanaged';[55] that many people in Washington might be good people, but the system was 'rotten';[56] that laws were passed not by members of Congress, but through the pressures of lawyers and lobbyists;[57] and that the mess in Washington needed to be cleaned up[58] legitimized the nation's concerns. His 30-minute infomercials also invoked and played out this myth. The infomercials were composed of short segments – or what might be called 'adlets' – in which Perot, pointer in hand and graphs and charts on display, catalogued the nation's ills.

Individual occurrences during the campaign gave credence to Perot's lamentations, for example other candidates, taking up the typical challenger's role of calling for change, railed about a 'Santa Claus'[59] government dispensing largesse without thought of the consequences, a 'gridlocked' and divided government unable to make any headway toward legislation to cure domestic problems such as crime and health care, and an impotent government without the ability to stave off bad foreign trade agreements. Also, media, with their tendency to focus on candidates' strategies rather than the substance of their positions on individual issues, fueled the nation's cynicism and thus became a partner in underscoring the veracity of the myth. This myth alone, however, was not sufficient to warrant support for Perot. What made Perot's candidacy compelling for so many was the merger of this first myth with the second: the myth of the hero/outsider. This second myth was one for which Perot's background was more than adequately suited.

Perot seemed to be the embodiment of the proverbial rags to riches story.[60] His life seemed a catalog of successes – success in business, success in his family life, success as a contributing member of his community. He seemed to be his own man, not afraid to say what he thought needed saying and with the ability to cut through the trivial, the mundane and the unnecessarily complex and make things happen. He seemed to be what Walter Fisher had in mind in his essay on romantic democracy:

> A romantic figure need only be an adventurous, colorful, daring and impassioned exponent of certain American ideals, such as individualism, achievement, and success. To be an American hero, one must not only display these qualities, one must also be visionary and mythic, a subject for folklore and legend. The American hero evokes the image of the American Dream, of the ways people and things are when the spirit of America transcends the moment, and her destiny is manifest.[61]

For many, Perot's life story was reminiscent of legends of the old west: the good guy in the white hat, the sheriff vowing to uphold the moral good who would ride the villains out of town. After all, as Perot reminded voters, his nation and its citizens had called upon him many times to come to their aid and provide assistance they could not provide for themselves.[62] When his government was stymied by Iranian kidnappers, it was Perot who organized the release of hostages;[63] when a giant of American capitalism, General Motors, faced economic problems, it was Perot who had done everything he could 'to get General Motors to face its problems'.[64]

Also, like the sagacious sheriff, he knew what had to be done and wasted no time in the doing: 'I'm results oriented. I am action oriented. I've dealt with my businesses. Getting things done in three months that my competitors took 18 months to do'.[65] For citizens who saw their government suffering from inertia, lumbering along aimlessly and accomplishing little, Perot seemed the perfect antidote. He presented himself as the consummate outsider free of entangling alliances who could represent their concerns and voice their complaints. In his book *The Hero in America*, Dixon Wector describes the hero as

> an index to the collective mind and heart. His deeds and qualities are those which millions endorse. He speaks words that multitudes want said; he stands for things that they are often willing to spill their blood for. The hero is he whom every American should wish to be. His legend is the mirror of the folk soul.[66]

For many, Ross Perot was such a hero. The merger of the myth of hobbled government and the myth of the hero/outsider produced a narrative that was pervasive in Perot's campaign: he was the hero/outsider who possessed the ability to set right our government. It is this intersection of fact and fiction that provides a comfortable familiarity for citizens and which, as familiarity does, introduces order into what otherwise might seem chaotic. The narrative is, in the communication theorist Kenneth Burke's terms, a 'repetitive form', a 'consistent maintaining of a principle under new guises', a 'restatement of the same thing in different ways', a 'restatement of a theme by new details'.[67] Because Perot's story is both internally and externally consistent, that is, it possesses, in Fisher's terms, fidelity and probability and therefore seems credible given what we think to be true, it results in a compelling characterization of Perot which argues strongly on his behalf. Moreover the story in its consistency has the capacity to insulate Perot from criticism. It is, after all, difficult to criticize the central figure in such a time-honored and venerated narrative and one that is grounded in moral inducement: the objective of achieving the good. The narrative, then, becomes the backdrop for Perot's campaign, the compass which directs understandings of him and his actions. Each new piece of information is assessed on the basis of its consistency with the story; the narrative serves as anchor for perceptions and evaluations of Ross Perot.

Common Sense

To the degree that the two remaining strategies function effectively, they do so because they are understood in light of and measured against the structure of the narrative. In the first of these two strategies, Perot, as the hero/outsider, employs reductionist and synecdochic language strategies to set up an enthymemetic relationship with his audience.[68] Typically, he will suggest that complex problems can be addressed and remedied through the application of a quality 'the people' possess and of which government officials have lost sight: common sense. For example a metaphor which equates a complex governmental problem with the simplicity of a machine in need of repair reduces the problem's complexity and defines and confines the range of possible solutions. Having reduced the complex argument to the simple, Perot offers the same metaphor as emblematic of all complex governmental problems. If all problems can be solved so easily, all one presumably needs to do is use common sense. Thus he elicits a completion or conclusion of his enthymeme on the part of his listeners. They are taught to regard, for example, the fiscal and ethical issues in their own lives as simple and responsive to principles that are comfortably familiar; then the simplicities of their own lives are made to stand in for the complexities of national politics.

In the first of the three nationally televised debates, for example, Perot asserts that 'there are great plans lying all over Washington nobody ever uses. It's like having a blueprint for a house you never built'.[69] In the second of the televised debates, he returns to the question of plans for solving and alleviating problems and declares that '[e]verybody knows how to fix them. There are people all over the federal government, if they could just touch it with a screwdriver, could fix it'.[70] A similar metaphor he often uses for solving problems is to 'get under the hood' and get the car (government) running smoothly again. The blueprint is equated with plans for solving national dilemmas and the screwdriver and the mechanic repairing the car are equated with the process necessary to implement those plans; through the metaphors, problems and their solutions are reduced to the simple and the solvable, readily apparent to anyone who has the common sense to see them. When the hearer allows simplicities to stand in for complexities, she or he joins and completes the argument enthymemetically.

The question which surely arises is this: how could an audience accept this reductionist perspective? Did they not conceive of Perot's strategies as amateurish at best and ill-informed at worst? What allows an audience member or voter to accept this strategy, a strategy which permeates Perot's rhetoric, is an unreflective recognition of the familiar quality of common sense. Fisher, along with others,[71] argues that narrative, in its assumption of a base of knowledge shared by the audience, is the primary conveyor of common sense. Moreover, as Fisher says, this common-sense knowledge is typically expressed as the opposite of 'elitist' or 'technical' knowledge, and because common sense is self-evident, it is insulated against indictments leveled by those who profess expertise.[72] Thus, when Perot proclaims that the 'we' who will govern means 'you and me', he aligns himself with the people and creates the illusion of self-evident truth in opposition to elite and technical knowledge. Although Perot says that, as president, he will bring in the 'experts' (usually described as 'world-class' experts) to work on a problem, he clearly implies that one need not be an expert or even understand the mysteries to which the experts are privy to engage in the process of solving problems; one need only do what any reasonable, commonsensical person would do.[73]

This line of 'reasoning' becomes particularly powerful for two reasons. First, the use of the metaphor and the appeal to common sense are contextualized by the dominant and consistent narrative of Perot as hero/outsider tackling governmental problems. When assessed in light of the narrative, the metaphorical argument takes on a patina of logic in that it seems reasonable to conclude that the hero, imbued with insight and wisdom, can surely understand, make sense of and bring order to the chaotic. Second, when any rhetor makes use of the device of the enthymeme, he or she invites the audience to become a willing participant in the creation of an argument. Through the use of the metaphorically-based enthymeme, Perot co-opts his audience and its shared belief in common sense and makes it an accomplice in crafting his argument. For an audience of citizen-voters already angered by feelings of detachment and powerlessness, this process is powerful in its ability to provide an opportunity for their renewed participation. Participation in the argument *about* their government is, after all, better than no participation at all, and may even be viewed as one step closer to renewed participation *in* their government.

We Need More Action

The last of the three rhetorical strategies used by Ross Perot is rooted in his argument that public officials have engaged in too much talk and not enough action. While his call for action is compelling to a nation not enamored of a democracy's inherent qualities of discussion and incrementalism as a path toward decision and action, many citizens still recognize the need for deliberation. Through specific language choices, Perot creates the illusion that he possesses or has provided his audience with essential information, as well as the illusion that deliberation has already occurred; he then invites the audience to agree upon a movement to action. The result is often the acceptance by his audience of a fallacious argument.

A central tenet of Perot's political rhetoric is the need for less talk and more action. He describes himself as someone who is experienced in 'not taking 10 years to solve a 10-minute problem'.[74] Clearly this appeal to the urgency of action is meant to contrast with and build from the nation's shared perception of a 'gridlocked' and immobilized government. Clearly, too, the call for action is given force by the narrative: the hero is not predisposed to sit about and talk; his natural disposition prizes action. But for citizens schooled in representative democracy, deliberation is understood as a prerequisite for action, regardless of how compelling the notion of action may seem. Even Perot urges prior deliberation in his use of the, once again, commonsensical adage: 'Like the old carpenter says: Measure twice, cut once'.[75] Having conceded that prior deliberation is necessary, Perot introduces the third rhetorical strategy: the illusion that sufficient information has been presented and that deliberation has occurred or will occur. He accomplishes this strategy in several ways.

First, his infomercials and campaign advertisements suggest that he is imparting information and allowing time for deliberation. The infomercials largely consisted of Perot's lengthy descriptions of the nation's problems illustrated through the use of graphs and charts, and offered very little in the way of solutions. A typical infomercial included some ten to twelve segments, each devoted to a particular topic. By the conclusion of the 30-minute infomercial, audiences may sense that a great deal of information has come their way. Volume alone (that is, thirty minutes as opposed to the usual thirty seconds of a political commercial, and ten to twelve segments each loaded with graphics and explanations) can convey a sense of substance, a sense that vast quantities of information have been provided. Additionally, the infomercials always featured Perot in a business-like setting, seated at a desk with visual aids ready for display. Not only does this setting suggest deliberation, insofar as it shows Perot taking the time to sit and talk to the people about their nation, but it may well carry the additional advantage of providing viewers with visual cues that they associate with presidential addresses broadcast from the White House's Oval Office. In one sense, Perot's infomercials gave his audience the sense of what Perot as president might look like.

The shorter, standard-length campaign advertisements Perot used also suggest deliberation and the imparting of information. Typically, Perot's advertisements featured somber background music with a male voice-over reading text that simultaneously scrolled across the screen from bottom to top. The written text, underscored and reinforced by voice, and the screen, constantly filled with words against a background of music and pictures that could magnify the import of the words, potentially prime viewers to conclude that a large quantity of information is being conveyed. The multiple levels of two different channels of communication, that is, visual and aural, create this sense. Moreover the advertisements consistently exhibited a quiet, contemplative tone as though viewers were being invited to take a moment from their busy schedules and consider the problems of their nation. When one of these ads was aired, its quiet and contemplative tone stood in sharp contrast to the visually dramatic and active commercial advertisements which surrounded it, thus amplifying its deliberative tone.

A second way in which Perot suggests the presence of information and deliberation can be traced to two recurring and interdependent features of his rhetoric. Often Perot moved swiftly through his explanation of the process he would use to solve problems. In an essay on Perot published by *National Review*, Amherst College professor Hadley Arkes provides an example of this first feature:

> Larry King had the impression that Perot was 'pro gun control', but Perot quickly rejoined, 'No. Now wait a minute.' He was in favor of certain controls, but not for everyone. 'When I was a boy in Texas,' said Perot, 'we all had guns but we didn't shoot one another … The problem is to get the guns out of the hands of the violent people.' King naturally wished to know just how Perot would identify those 'violent people'. Well, Perot explained, you start like this: 'Bring together law-enforcement officers, the district attorneys, the judges, National Rifle Association, all these different groups who I already know from conversation with them say, "Yes. We will go to the wall with you to get guns out of the hands of violent people." Then we'll develop a plan to do that. Then we go through television through the

Town Hall. We explain that to the American people. We build a consensus. We pass the laws and we move on [to] the next problem.'[76]

The quick move from problem to imagined yet unstated solution supports Perot's call for less talk and more action. But if we think that he has glossed over the difficult parts of this process, that is, getting the experts and the people to consider the problem and come to consensus on the solutions, the second feature of his rhetoric functions to provide assurance of his abilities. Perot peppers his speech with a rhetorical device that suggests organizational and leadership abilities on his part. That device is the numbering of ideas. For example, when asked in the first presidential debate what the United States can do to defend its national interests, Perot responds by using the numerical device to list his ideas and employs it again in his summary when he says,

So, in terms of priorities, we've got to be financially strong. Number two, we've got to take care of this missile situation and try to get the nuclear war behind us and give that a very high priority. And number three, we need to help and support Russia and the republics in every possible way to become democratic, capitalistic societies.[77]

Throughout the debates, the infomercials and his appearances on talk shows, Perot laced his comments with the numbering of ideas. The power of this device is located in its suggestion that the rhetorician must possess information and that prior deliberation on this information must have occurred to permit him to enumerate his conclusions about the information. Despite the fact that, when one scans the entirety of Perot's answer to the question put to him in the debate, no evidence exists of how he would implement his plan, the use of the numbering suggests that he has deliberated on this issue. When the quick movement through a problem and 'solution' is coupled with what appears to be organized elaboration on the problem and 'solution', the inference may be drawn that information is present and deliberation has occurred.

The final way in which Perot suggests information and deliberation is through the use of words or phrases that trigger

the inference to that end. For example Perot will introduce
an issue and, after spending a brief space of time seeming to
talk about the issue, he will interject the word 'now' and then
proceed. The interjection of 'now' suggests that what has
come before was contextual, setting the stage for the specific
answer to come. What follows 'now', though, often is no more
specific and usually evades the question altogether; in fact
occasionally what follows 'now' is a shift to an entirely different subject. An illustration is found in the second presidential
debate. In his response to a question asking how 'in specific
dollar goals' the deficit should be reduced, Perot responds in
this way:

> Well, we're $4 trillion in debt. We're going into debt an
> additional $1 billion, a little more than $1 billion every
> working day of the year.
>
> *Now*, the thing I love about it – I'm just a businessman. I
> was down in Texas taking care of business, tending to my
> family. This situation got so bad that I decided I'd better get
> into it. The American people asked me to get into it. But I
> just find it fascinating that while we sit here tonight we will
> go into debt an additional $50 million in an hour and a
> half.
>
> *Now*, it's not the Republicans' fault, of course, and it's not
> the Democrats' fault. And what I'm looking for is, who did
> it? *Now*, they're the two folks involved so maybe if you put
> them together, they did it.
>
> *Now*, the facts are we have to fix it. I'm here tonight for
> these young people up here in the balcony from this
> college. When I was a young man, when I got out of the
> Navy, I had multiple job offers. Young people with high
> grades can't get a job. People – the 18- to 24-year-old high
> school graduates 10 years ago were making more than they
> are now. In other words, we were down to 18 per cent of
> them were making – 18- to 24-year-olds were making less
> than $12,000. Now that's up to 40 per cent. And what's
> happened in the meantime? The dollar's gone through the
> floor.
>
> *Now* whose fault is that? Not the Democrats. Not the
> Republicans. Somewhere out there there's an extraterres-
> trial that's doing this to us, I guess. And everybody says they

take responsibility for this. Somebody somewhere has to take responsibility for this.

Put it to you bluntly, American people. If you want me to be your president, we're going to face our problems. We'll solve our problems. We'll pay down our debt. We'll pass on the American dream to our children, and I will not leave our children a situation that they have today.

When I was a boy, it took two generations to double the standard of living. Today it will take 12 generations. Our children will not see the American dream because of this debt that somebody somewhere dropped on us[78] [emphasis added].

Each use of 'now' has the potential to trigger in the audience the inference that information has been or will be provided. Moreover the consecutive uses of 'now' imply that prior deliberation has occurred on Perot's part and that he is dissecting the problem and presenting its component parts for the audience members' benefit, so that the audience might follow his 'logic'.

Perot's answer also includes another example of inferential triggering: 'Now, the thing I love about it...' The phrases 'The thing I love about it', 'I just love the fact that' and 'I just find it fascinating', or variations of those phrases, are found throughout Perot's speech. In general the phrases function rhetorically to place Perot in a superior position, a position from which he has the unique ability to see what others cannot. Simultaneously the phrases diminish and demean the positions of others. Beyond this general function, the phrases suggest one of at least two messages: (1) while others are focused on the trivial, Perot and his supporters are focused on important concerns; or (2) others (and most often he means politicians, special interests, and the media) are conspiring to advantage themselves at the expense of 'the people'. In the third presidential debate, Perot says

I just love the fact that everybody, particularly in the media, goes bonkers over the town hall. I guess it's because you will lose your right to tell them [the people] what to think. The point is, they'll get to decide what to think.

I love the fact that people will listen to a guy with a bad accent and a poor presentation manner talking about flip

charts for 30 minutes, because they want the details. See, all
the folks up there at the top said the attention span of the
American people is no more than five minutes, they won't
watch it. They're thirsty for it[79] [emphasis added].

The use of 'I just love the fact that' prompts the inference
that, while others – and in particular the media – are invested
in controlling and influencing available information, Perot is
dedicated to ensuring that information is made available to
voters and that Perot, on the contrary, is providing opportunities (for example, through the infomercials) for discussing
that information. Responding to a question about health care
reform in the third debate, Perot says

> *It's fascinating.* You've bought a front-row box seat and
> you're not happy with your health care and you're saying
> tonight we've got bad health care but very expensive health
> care. Folks, here's why. Go home and look in the mirror.
> You own this country, but you have no voice in it the way
> it's organized now, and if you want to have a high-risk expe-
> rience, comparable to bungee jumping, go into Congress
> some time when they're working on this kind of legislation,
> when the lobbyists are running up and down the halls. Wear
> your safety toe shoes when you go. And as a private citizen,
> believe me, you are looked on as a major nuisance[80]
> [emphasis added].

In this example the use of 'it's fascinating' not only leads to
the inference that Perot is in an advantaged position from
which he is privy to peculiar insights, but also paves the way for
the subsequent assertion that those in Washington, in their
self-interested zeal, are not at all concerned with the public
being informed, and in fact find the public a 'nuisance', an
impediment. The implied conclusion is that, unlike those currently in power, Perot is interested in providing information
and in engaging in discussion.

Predictably, variations on these phrases appeared in remarks
at a press conference Perot called on 26 October to respond
to questions about his allegations that the Bush campaign had
attempted 'dirty tricks' to derail Perot's campaign. The statement 'I find it fascinating that you, that CNN, would run a
story this morning, wondering why I brought it up yesterday at
the last minute'[81] suggests a conspiracy on the media's part to

disparage and embarrass, and thus silence, Perot. Later in that same news conference Perot wondered aloud why the Bush administration never contacted him to deny the allegations and turned the tables with variations of the phrase: 'Don't you find it strange that at the highest levels of the administration nobody ever called me back and said, "Ross, this didn't happen"?... Does anybody here not find it interesting that they never called back and said it's not true?' The phrases again evoke the inference of conspiracy and serve as an appeal to understand Perot as the victim of those who would silence his attempts to engage in the deliberation over important issues.

In summary, the infomercials and campaign advertisements, the rhetorical device of enumerating ideas and the phrases which trigger inferential conclusions all suggest that information has been or will be presented and that deliberation has occurred or is occurring. Their cumulative effect is a rhetorical strategy that the narrative underscores and to which it gives credibility. It is the familiar story line of the insightful and untainted hero waging war against the deceitful and manipulative foe; it is the story of the hero prepared for appropriate action and yet tempered by wisdom and experience.

The rhetorical strategies used by Ross Perot converged to form a message that prompted different responses to his candidacy. For some voters Perot's candidacy was emblematic of change, a change that would restore order to a government in disarray, renew the commitment of public officials to serving the best interests of the nation and reclaim for citizens their rightful place as 'owners' of the country. For others Perot's candidacy was compelling in that it exemplified an expression of the nation's dissatisfaction; however it offered no stable or viable alternative. And for still others Perot's candidacy represented nothing more than empty populist appeals that substituted high emotion for reasoned argument and quick action for sound deliberation. The question that remains is this: what made Perot's candidacy the relative success that it was?

DESPITE FAILURE: THE SUCCESS OF THE PEROT CAMPAIGN

Throughout the September 1994 American Political Science Association convention in Washington, DC, scholars offered various perspectives in an attempt to evaluate the presidency of Bill Clinton. One theme that emerged from those attempts was that rhetorical exigencies at the presidential level had changed and that, to be effective, presidential rhetoric must be transformed to meet those new exigencies. David Broder attended that convention, and in his column in *The Washington Post* summarized and commented on the reason for that needed transformation:

> The modern presidency was built on crises – first the Depression, then World War II and then the Cold War – into something far larger than the Constitution envisaged. With the United States now the sole military superpower, the presidency is a less grandiose office ... Neither the press nor the president has adapted to this change. Presidents still seek to dramatize themselves as prime movers of events, making exaggerated promises in the campaign and launching overblown initiatives once in office. We in the media feed this narcissism by focusing on the White House as if it were the great locus of power in our Republic.[82]

Thus when President George Bush declared an end to the Cold War, no crisis of a similar magnitude existed. With the Bush declaration, not only did the United States no longer face a major crisis, it also no longer faced a great enemy against which the nation's citizens could unite. The task for President Clinton, the scholars suggested, is to move beyond the crisis rhetoric of the Cold War and craft a new rhetoric, one that addresses new and different concerns in new and different ways. I agree with those scholars, but would add that the need for this new rhetoric did not surface with the inauguration of Bill Clinton. The first instance of the need for this new rhetoric took place in the 1992 presidential campaign, and the candidacy of Ross Perot derived a great deal of its headway with voters from his ability to move toward a new rhetoric.

Lacking a national crisis and an enemy against which to unite citizens, all three major candidates for office created a new crisis and a new enemy. In one form or another, politics and government were inextricably linked and were made indistinguishable from one another to become politics/government, the new enemy. Not only was this a consistent message among the three candidates, but also the message was reinforced by criticisms of politics and government leveled by the media.[83] Given the mood of the electorate, this message played well. For citizens feeling frustration and alienation, this new enemy that combined popular notions of self-serving politicians and unresponsive government provided a concrete target for their anger.

For Bill Clinton, politics/government, as such, was not a problem; rather, he argued, what politics/government had become under twelve years of Republication administrations was the problem. It had, Clinton argued, lost touch with citizens, become prodigal, and treated unfairly those 'who do the work, pay the taxes, raise the kids and play by the rules'.[84] For a challenger to link politics and government and assert that the two had become a single enemy might not have seemed all that unusual; challengers from the major opposing party typically argue (some with more hyperbole than others) that those in office should be replaced because they had squandered the trust placed in them and corrupted the governing system. And yet, for Clinton to formulate this argument may have seemed self-serving to some citizens, for after all he was a politician and had spent a great deal of his life in government. Those who felt deeply cynical about politics and government and powerless to effect change may have wondered how someone who had been a part of the political system could be expected to alter the system. For those citizens, politics and government are the same regardless of their location in the state's capital or the nation's capital.

President George Bush also linked politics and government and made them an enemy; in his case, though, only some of the politicians and only one part of government were the villain: the Democrat-controlled Congress. In two of his major addresses during the campaign year, the 1992 State of the Union and his acceptance speech at the August Republican convention, and throughout his campaign as well, Bush denounced Congress and made it his (and our) enemy, an enemy with whom he relished 'a good fight'.[85] Some citizens might certainly have reasoned that Bush had had his opportunity in four years of office to slay that dragon and had failed; why give him another chance?

Ross Perot clearly had politics/government in mind as the enemy, an enemy that had, he implied, obdurately neglected and forgotten those it should have served. For many citizens Perot might have been the only candidate who could, with any sense of legitimacy, make the argument that politics/government was the enemy, for he was the only major candidate who had not held an elected public office and thus could claim not to be any part of the problem.

Making politics/government the enemy, though, is only part of the explanation of Perot's relative success in garnering significant support without the imprimatur of a major political party. Voters seek a candidate who not only seems to understand 'the problem', but also seems to have 'a solution', one that is central to the candidate's vision for the future of the nation. Bush's solution was an electoral one: change the majority party in the House and Senate from Democrat to Republican and return Bush to office. Moreover Bush may have given evidence for voters' concerns about him by his admission that he didn't do 'the vision thing' well. Clinton's solution came in the form of a 'new covenant' he would craft, 'a solemn commitment between the people and their government'.[86] For some citizens, this joining with the enemy might not have sounded appealing.

Perot's approach to 'the solution' was decidedly different from the approaches of Bush and Clinton. For Perot 'the solution' lay not in any vision he would provide; rather, with his admonition that government should come 'from the people' and not 'at the people', Perot located both solution and vision in the people. How would this vision be carried out? The answer to that question lay in what many citizens might have seen as a futuristic, even visionary mechanism for subjugating the enemy, politics/government: the technological conduit of the town hall. The people would make their wishes known and express their vision, and Perot, as their 'servant', would carry out those wishes and that vision. As he often reminded voters (in an appeal rooted in the strategy of personal identification), 'I'm Ross and you're the boss'. Locating vision in the people provided a fourfold advantage for Perot. First, it was a flattering appeal to voters to be told that they (more so than politicians and even Perot himself) were the repository of a vision for the nation's future. Second, it played into and reinforced the legitimacy of voters' sense of alienation and the need for a different kind of candidate. Third, it supplied citizens with the vehicle for becoming participants rather than spectators in their governance. And fourth, by implication, Perot himself could be seen as visionary for having conceived and proposed the mechanism through which citizens could defuse the power of politicians and reclaim their government – the town hall.

To the extent that Perot's candidacy was a success, it was so because he was able to locate and articulate the concerns and frustrations of the nation in a more internally consistent message than his opponents offered. For Clinton the solution to the problem of politics/government as enemy was a 'new covenant', a different connection, but a connection nonetheless, between the people and politics/government. For George Bush the solution to the problem of politics/government was to elect different politicians. In both cases, however, the potential for the survival of the nemesis politics/government remained, though it might survive in altered form. For Perot the solution to the problem lay in a promise not to reform but to revolutionize, that is, to replace the power and decision-making abilities of politics/government with the power and decision-making abilities of the people. Combining the depiction of politics/government as the enemy and Perot as the only legitimate outsider who could successfully overcome that enemy with the message of revolution rather than reform provided Perot's message an internal consistency clearly compelling to many citizens. It struck the chord of a new rhetoric to many who felt alienated and powerless in a post-Cold War nation poised for a new message. The advisability of that new rhetoric is another question.

CONCLUSION

Central to Ross Perot's campaign message was the argument that, if we could just take politics out of politics and substitute it with a clearly heard and quickly heeded voice of the people, the nation's problems could be solved. An analysis and understanding of Perot's antipolitical rhetoric as containing this central message prompt two precautions citizens should take in assessing such rhetoric. First, we should remind ourselves of the inherent differences between direct democracy and representative democracy. Perot's call for a more direct voice of the people has the potential to confuse the two forms and undermine the system of representative democracy without offering evidence to substantiate a preference for its alternative. Following this line of reasoning, Harvey Mansfield argues that 'it is just this confusion – the ever present demon of popular government – that Perot promises to embrace. He will be the servant of the people who acts, moves, executes on their behalf. Docile to them, he will be decisive for them; and they, in turn will rule by being ruled'.[87] The assertion that more direct democracy is preferable to the nation's current representative system is a claim that confronts and questions the foundation upon which the nation was conceived and has existed. To make this claim or even imply this claim requires that the rhetorician be held accountable for the claim and produce sound argument and reasoned justification for its acceptance.

The second precaution citizens should take in assessing such rhetoric relates to the conception of government as gridlocked and slow to respond. In the first presidential debate, Perot spoke to that conception and repeated a theme pervasive in his campaign: 'Talk is cheap. Words are plentiful. Deed are precious. Let's get on with it'.[88] We should remind ourselves that essential to democracy (and, more specifically, to a representative democracy) is the opportunity and necessity for deliberation. To advocate replacing talk with action is to advocate replacing deliberation with a speedy adherence to the people's wishes. Ultimately such a claim results in the devaluing of talk, the distinctive medium of all politics, and particularly of democratic politics.

Notes

1. S. V. Roberts, 'The Mood Swings of Anxious Voters', *U.S. News and World Report*, 24 August 1992, p. 32.
2. Ibid., pp. 32–4. See also D. Balz, 'Voters Seek Plain Talk about the Big Issues', *The Washington Post*, 8 March 1992, p. A1; D. Wessel, 'Taking the Pulse', *The Wall Street Journal*, 5 March 1992, p. A1.
3. G. Wills, 'The Power of the Savior', *Time*, 22 June 1992, pp. 41–2.
4. H. Mansfield, 'Only Amend', *The New Republic*, 6 July 1992, p. 14.
5. D. Balz, 'A Year Later, Perot's Purpose Still Defies Definition', *The Washington Post*, 22 June 1993, p. A1.
6. D. Balz, 'Perot Avoids Specifying Spending He'd Reduce to Balance the Budget', *The Washington Post*, 3 August 1993, p. A8.

7. A. Devroy, 'Perot Takes Early Lead in Race on Trade Pact', *The Washington Post,* 26 August 1993, p. A12. See also D. S. Hilzenrath, 'Administration Accuses Perot of Spreading NAFTA Falsehoods', *The Washington Post,* 3 September 1993, p. A11.

8. D. S. Broder, 'Tuesday Night Food Fight', *The Washington Post,* 11 November 1993, p. A23.

9. T. B. Edsall, 'Perot Backs Spending Cuts', *The Washington Post,* 22 April 1994, p. A22. See also E. Pianin 'Perot Launches Bid to Sway Upcoming Elections', *The Washington Post,* 11 September 1994, p. A8.

10. S. Wilentz, 'Pox Populi', *The New Republic,* 9 August 1993, p. 29.

11. K. Burke, *A Grammar of Motives* (Berkeley, Cal.: University of California Press, 1969), p. 472.

12. J. Byrd, 'Three Months of Ross Perot', *The Washington Post,* 19 July 1992, p. C6.

13. See J. B. Judis, 'Bill Folds', *The New Republic,* 28 January 1991, pp. 17–20; E Clift, 'Challengers on Ice', *Newsweek,* 7 January 1991, p. 30; M. Greenfield, 'The Dropout Democrats', *Newsweek,* 16 September 1991, p. 72; M. Kondracke, 'Gun Shy', *The New Republic,* 20 May 1991, pp. 19–20; A. McCarthy, 'Wanted: Sacrificial Lamb', *Commonweal,* 12 July 1992, pp. 422–3.

14. As early as mid-May 1991 the president's approval ratings had begun to drop and yet registered at a quite respectable 74 per cent. See 'Bush in Latest Poll', *The Wall Street Journal,* 16 May 1991, p. A16. However by the end of 1991, the year in which he had presided over the liberation of Kuwait and declared a 'New World Order', Bush's approval rating had moved to the lowest point of his presidency: 47 per cent. See R. Morin and D. Balz, 'Bush Approval Rating Slips to 47%', *The Washington Post,* 17 December 1991, p. A1.

15. J. Nelson, 'Poll Finds Bush's Approval Rating at 39%', *Los Angeles Times,* 28 February 1992, p. A36.

16. M. Shields, 'The Gulf Glow Fades', *The Washington Post,* 6 March 1992, p. A23.

17. M. Williams, 'What We Know About George', *The Washington Post Magazine,* 16 August 1992, p. 10.

18. For a more complete picture of the Democratic contenders, see G. M. Pomper (ed.), *The Election of 1992* (Chatham, NJ: Chatham House, 1993).

19. See G. Will, 'A Figure of Genuine Pathos', *The Washington Post,* 29 July 1992, p. A23.

20. C. Krauthammer, 'The Swoon for Tycoons', *The Washington Post,* 12 June 1992, p. A23.

21. D. S. Broder, 'When Winning Isn't Everything', *The Washington Post National Weekly Edition,* 8–14 June 1992.

22. Wills, op. cit., p. 41.

23. See, for example, J. Mintz, 'Crusades of Ross Perot', *The Washington Post,* 24 April 1992, p. A1.

24. J. Ceaser and A. Busch, *Upside Down and Inside Out: The 1992 Election and American Politics* (Lanham, Md: Rowman and Littlefield, 1993), pp. 90–1.

25. See, for example, J. Solomon, 'Nixon Administration Documents Show Perot as Ultimate Insider', *The Washington Post*, 8 May 1992, p. A4; D. Rogers and J. Abramson, 'Ross Perot Takes Surveillance Tactics to Unusual Lengths', *The Wall Street Journal*, 12 June 1992, p. A1.

26. D. Shribman, 'H. Ross Perot Vies for Disaffected Voters in Bid For Presidency', *The Wall Street Journal*, 9 April 1992, p. A1.

27. D. Shribman, 'Ross Perot, Though To Many A Political Unknown, Emerges in Polls As A Formidable But Elusive Force', *The Wall Street Journal*, 16 April 1992, p. A26.

28. D. Shribman, 'Voters Who Know A Lot About Him Often Favor Perot', *The Wall Street Journal*, 22 May 1992, p. A4.

29. B. McAllister and R. Marcus, 'Presidential Race Looks Tighter', *The Washington Post*, 25 October 1992, p. A1.

30. 'Transcript of the First Presidential Debate', *The Washington Post*, 12 October 1992, p. A18.

31. 'Transcript of the Second Presidential Debate', *The Washington Post*, 16 October 1992, p. A34.

32. 'First Presidential Debate', op. cit., p. A17.

33. 'Second Presidential Debate', op. cit., p. A36.

34. P. Milius, 'Perot's Fuzz', *The Washington Post*, 4 May 1992, p. A23.

35. 'First Presidential Debate', op. cit., p. A16.

36. 'Transcript of the Third Presidential Debate', *The Washington Post*, 20 October 1992, p. A25.

37. 'First Presidential Debate', op. cit., p. A18.

38. M. Isikoff, 'Perot Plans to Mobilize His Volunteers As a New Force in American Politics', *The Washington Post*, 18 July 1992, p. A11.

39. Ibid.

40. Ibid.

41. J. Mintz, 'Dirty Tricks Charged by Perot', *The Washington Post*, 26 October 1992, p. A9.

42. 'Third Presidential Debate', op. cit., p. A24.

43. K. Hall Jamieson, 'The Subversive Effects of a Focus on Narrative Strategy in News Coverage of Presidential Campaigns', in *1-800-PRESIDENT: The Report of the Twentieth Century Fund Task Force on Television and the Campaign of 1992* (Washington, DC The Brookings Institution, 1993), p. 38.

44. 'Third Presidential Debate', op. cit., p. A24.

45. Ibid., pp. A24–5.

46. 'First Presidential Debate', op. cit., p. A16.

47. Ceaser and Busch, op. cit., pp. 102–4.

48. T. Shales, 'Uncanned Ham: Perot's Shows', *The Washington Post*, 27 October 1992, p. C8.

49. W. Croty (ed.), *America's Choice: The Election of 1992* (Guildford, Conn.: The Dushkin Publishing Group, 1993), p. 1.

50. F. McDonald, *The American Presidency: An Intellectual History* (Lawrence, Kans.: University Press of Kansas, 1994), p. 417.

51. 'A synecdoche is a trope, which puts the name of the whole for the part, or the name of the part for the whole.' L. Thonssen, A. C. Baird,

and W. W. Braden, *Speech Criticism* (Malabar, Fla: Robert E. Krieger Publishing, 1981), p. 503. The enthymeme is a form of proof that 'draws conclusions from admitted propositions' (ibid., p. 70).

52. W. R. Fisher, 'Narration as a Human Communication Paradigm: The Case of Public Moral Argument', *Communication Monographs*, vol. 51 (1984), p. 2.
53. Ibid., p. 8.
54. Ibid., p. 4.
55. 'First Presidential Debate', op. cit., p. A16.
56. 'Second Presidential Debate', op. cit., p. A35.
57. 'Third Presidential Debate', op. cit., p. A23.
58. 'First Presidential Debate', op. cit., p. A16.
59. The phrase 'no more Santa Claus' originated with Paul Tsongas early in the primaries; Perot later adopted its use.
60. P. Richter, 'Perot Runs Biographical Infomercial', *Los Angeles Times*, 23 October 1992, p. A20.
61. W. R. Fisher, 'Romantic Democracy, Ronald Reagan, and Presidential Heroes', *Western Journal of Speech Communication* (1982), p. 301.
62. 'Third Presidential Debate', p. A22.
63. S. Blumenthal, 'Perotnoia', *The New Republic*, 15 June 1992, p. 23.
64. 'Third Presidential Debate', op. cit., p. A22.
65. 'Second Presidential Debate', op. cit., p. A37.
66. D. Wector, *The Hero in America* (Ann Arbor, Mich.: University of Michigan Press, 1941), p. 488.
67. K. Burke, *Counter-Statement*, 3rd edn (Berkeley, Cal.: University of California Press, 1968), p. 125.
68. On synecdoches and enthymemes, see note 51 above.
69. 'First Presidential Debate', op. cit., p. A17.
70. 'Second Presidential Debate', op. cit., p. A36.
71. L. O. Mink, 'Narrative Form as a Cognitive Instrument', in R. H. Canary and H. Kozicki (eds) *The Writing of History*, (Madison, Wis.: University of Wisconsin Press, 1978).
72. Fisher, 'Narration as a Human Communication Paradigm', op. cit., p. 9.
73. Perot's contempt for expertise in political life is emblematic of one strain of modern liberalism since its inception. Hobbes reduced the classical virtue of prudence from its status as the distinctive mark of rulers to merely the accumulation of commonsense experience. Thus '[t]o govern well a family, and a kingdom, are not different degrees of prudence; but different sorts of business... . A plain husbandman is more prudent in affairs of his own house, than a privy-councillor in the affairs of another man'. This was one of the essential grounds of Hobbes's doctrine of equality: 'For prudence is but experience; which equal time, equally bestows on all men... . [Men have] a vain conceit of [their] own wisdom', which results in the fact that 'howsoever they may acknowledge many others to be more witty, or more eloquent, or more learned; yet they will hardly believe there be many so wise as themselves...' T. Hobbes, *Leviathan*, ed. M. Oakeshott (New York: Collier Macmillan, 1962), pp. 61–2, 98. Tocqueville observed that this

grounding of the doctrine of equality in the common sense of the common man was central to the authority of the people in democratic regimes: 'The moral authority of the majority is partly based on the notion that there is more enlightenment and wisdom in a numerous assembly than in a single man ... It is the theory of equality applied to brains. This doctrine attacks the last asylum of human pride'. A. de Tocqueville, *Democracy in America*, ed. J. P. Mayer (Garden City, NY: Doubleday Anchor, 1969), p. 247.

74. 'First Presidential Debate', op. cit., p. A16.
75. 'Second Presidential Debate', op. cit., p. A36.
76. H. Arkes, 'The Man From Nowhere', *National Review*, 3 August 1992, p. 25.
77. 'First Presidential Debate', op. cit., p. A17.
78. 'Second Presidential Debate', op. cit., p. A34.
79. 'Third Presidential Debate', op. cit., p. A23.
80. 'Second Presidential Debate', op. cit., p. A35.
81. '"Nobody Ever Did Me the Courtesy to Call Back and Say ... We Didn't Do It"', *The Washington Post*, 27 October 1992, p. A12.
82. D. S. Broder, 'Boomer Bust: Why the Clinton/Quayle Generation Has A Problem Handling The Presidency', *The Washington Post*, 14 September 1992, p. A21. See also D. S. Broder, 'Presidential Scholars Grow Critical of Clinton's Performance in Office', *The Washington Post*, 4 September 1992, p. A10.
83. T. E. Patterson, *Out of Order* (New York: Vintage Books, 1994), p. 21.
84. B. Clinton, 'Acceptance Speech at Democratic Convention', *The Washington Post*, 17 July 1992, p. A26.
85. For the 28 January 1992 State of the Union address, see *The Washington Post*, 29 January 1992, p. A14. For the 20 August 1992 acceptance address at the Republican National Convention, see *Los Angeles Times*, 21 August 1992, p. A8.
86. Clinton, op. cit., p. A26.
87. Mansfield, op. cit., p. 14.
88. 'First Presidential Debate', op. cit., p. A19.

7 Markets versus Politics: On Globalization, Language and Legitimacy*

Louis Pauly

> What I mean by civilization, essentially, is language. One of the ways you can tell a civilization is in trouble is that the language is no longer used for communication, it is used for obscurantism, for control, for hiding things, and for secrecy.
> (John Ralston Saul)

The term 'antipolitics' covers a multitude of sins. Under this rubric, political scientists have analysed, among other things, the politics of neopopulist, oppositional and antiestablishment movements that are proliferating in so many countries around the world. As a scholar of international relations, it occurred to me that such movements and the oft-noted concern about states 'losing their sovereignty' in an era of sweeping economic and social change could be connected. This chapter is about that connection and the language used to obscure it.

The 'globalization of finance' is the latest jargon phrase used to connote a number of interrelated developments in the international economy. The most important include the reduction of direct controls and taxes on capital movements, the liberalization of long-standing regulatory restrictions within national financial markets, the expansion of lightly regulated 'offshore' financial markets and the introduction of new technologies in the process of financial intermediation. All of these developments render capital more mobile, both within and across national borders.

This chapter begins with an orientation to the central issue – international capital mobility. It focuses on the decontrol of short-term capital flows and is informed by relevant research

in international economics and international political
economy.[1] Much of the latter work treats capital mobility as a
dependent variable, and the most persuasive underlines the
deliberate policy choices of states under conditions of
tightening economic interdependence and rapid technological change.[2] A growing number of studies take the next logical
step and begin to probe the internal political contests behind
those choices. This has led others to reverse the causal chain
altogether and inquire into the internal and external political
implications of international capital mobility.[3] Such research
generally supports the view that its scale and durability
are now constitutive of a new regime in world politics, a
regime reasonably well established among advanced industrial
countries and spreading among others.

The chapter contends that this emergent regime of international capital mobility rests on flawed and potentially destab-
ilizing normative foundations. The core problem is one of
legitimacy, not autonomy. It can be rectified, but only if it is
first acknowledged. In the international arena, this is the
problem that lies behind misspecified fears concerning
nation-states 'losing their sovereignty'. In the domestic
realm, the problem may plausibly be related to the agendas
of populist political movements across a range of countries.
A short essay cannot do full justice to such themes. It can,
however, suggest that the policy trade-offs comprising the
normative underpinnings of the contemporary international monetary system require greater explication and
justification. The chapter concludes that the 'language' of
international capital mobility – the antipolitical language of
global market enthusiasts – obfuscates, but cannot solve, the
legitimacy problem.[4] The solution, like the problem, is inherently political.

THE NORMATIVE CONTEXT OF GLOBAL FINANCE

Conditions approximating what is now commonly, if hyper-
bolically, referred to as 'global finance' existed before 1914
among the most advanced economies and their dependencies.
The extremities of war and economic depression succeeded in
disrupting a system of economic adjustment that accommo-

dated, even necessitated, international capital flows. The system, which historians date from around 1870, rested on a normative consensus among the principal trading nations. At the center of that consensus lay a version of the gold standard, backed by the wealth and power of Great Britain.

The tumultuous era inaugurated in 1914 witnessed the rise and eventual economic dominance of the modern democratic nation-state, whose legitimacy ultimately depended on its ability to meet the expectations of its citizens in the twin realms of national economic welfare and national military security. Those expectations defined the terrain upon which the Bretton Woods system evolved after 1944, just as they lay behind the forces that eventually broke that system in the early 1970s.[5] The contemporary reconstruction of 'global' capital markets, or more precisely the dramatic expansion of international capital mobility, coincided with that breakdown and accelerated in its aftermath. The expectations of citizens concerning the responsibilities of democratic nation-states, however, have not substantively changed.[6]

Popular economic commentators, prominent bankers and true Marxists underscore the 'discipline' on autonomous state action implied by international capital mobility. Whether they embrace it or loathe it, they envisage the consolidation of a new global order, the borderless order of advanced capitalism. The vision is informed by a materialist worldview, and the language used to invoke it is the language of inevitability. Enjoining governments to yield to signals emanating from the 'global market', that language promotes a profound shift in policymaking authority. At the same time it appears to intentionally obscure the nature of that shift.

If sovereignty is defined as policy autonomy, which it commonly – and mistakenly – is, then international capital mobility by definition entails a loss of sovereignty. One problem is that this old chestnut ignores both an extensive literature on the evolution of the legal concept of sovereignty and a generation of research on the politics of international interdependence.[7] Another is that it downplays the stark historical lesson of 1914: under conditions of crisis, especially catastrophic crisis, the locus of ultimate political authority in the modern age – the state – is laid bare. But the most important problem is that it does nothing to help us understand the

actual situation we confront today at either the systemic or the
domestic level.

At the systemic level, the policy autonomy frame renders
important distinctions between states more difficult to assess.
Expanded capital mobility clearly constrains some states much
more than others, and in that difference resides power. This is
especially true when exchange rates are flexible and the dollar
remains the most common international medium of exchange, for example the United States is quite obviously less
constrained by capital mobility than states in the developing
world or, for that matter, than a number of its counterparts in
a not-yet-unified Europe.[8] At the domestic level, the policy
autonomy frame also does not allow us to see that international capital mobility has more disruptive consequences for
societies which are relatively rigidly organized and for particular groups within all societies. Such differences raise fundamental questions of justice. Although intuitively attractive, the
attempt to examine international capital mobility as a straightforward constraint on state autonomy misunderstands the
basic policy trade-offs behind it. Most problematically, it
obscures the historical fact that the promotion of capital
mobility by dominant states, and by dominant groups within
particular societies, has actually formed a key element of
strategies to maintain or regain policy autonomy.

If the more fundamental questions raised by the emergent
regime of international capital mobility are questions of relative power and justice, a more appropriate frame is provided
by the concept of legitimacy. That is to say, the core issue is
whether the *process* by which states have collectively devolved
power to international capital markets, and to those state and
non-state actors which hold dominant positions in those
markets, has been recognized by those whom it affects as
deserving of deference.[9] As a brief look back reveals, the
process has indeed fallen short of such a standard.

INTERNATIONAL CAPITAL MOBILITY IN RETROSPECT

The increasingly widespread belief that the holders of capital,
especially short-term or portfolio capital, have a right to move
it freely across national borders represents a distinct change in

the normative order originally crafted by leading states in the aftermath of the Second World War.[10] During the discussions leading up to the 1944 Bretton Woods Conference, one of the sticking points between the United States and Great Britain, the principal negotiators, involved the issue of official controls on short-term capital movements in a pegged exchange rate system. Although the chief British spokesman, John Maynard Keynes, had moved away from his own 1933 view that finance was not one of those 'things which should by their nature be international', he continued to believe strongly in the right of the individual state to impose capital controls as and when it alone perceived the need to arise.[11] The American position, articulated most forcefully by Harry Dexter White, approached the matter differently. Although willing to concede that 'disequilibrating' capital flows were both conceivable and undesirable, White envisaged a monetary order that would actively discourage all types of financial restrictions that impede trade and the international flow of 'productive' capital.[12] The word 'productive' here was carefully chosen; it was generally understood to distinguish such flows from 'speculative' flows.

The American position obviously reflected the expectation that, as the major creditor in the postwar order, the United States stood to benefit from as liberal an environment for international investment as it was possible to create. By the same token, however, the Americans were also intent on ensuring that access to the financial resources of the new international monetary institution they favored creating would be limited to countries facing temporary balance of payments problems; in the face of undesired capital outflows, the Americans preferred that a country undertake 'adjustment' (in its exchange rate and/or the domestic policies producing its payments problem) instead of seeking financing. They therefore contemplated a central regulatory role for the future International Monetary Fund (IMF).

In 1944 the final Bretton Woods compromise affirmed the priority of adjustment in the event of sustained capital outflows but left the option of controls to the discretion of individual states, provided only that such controls were not intended to restrict trade.[13] In the day-to-day experience of the IMF after its establishment, the difficulty of making clear distinctions between illegitimate 'exchange' restrictions and legitimate capital controls soon became apparent.[14] Among the leading industrial states, however, tensions related to such difficulties gradually began to ebb after the restoration of currency convertibility among the major industrial countries in 1958.

The ascendancy of capital mobility as a deliberate policy objective received limited expression in 1961 in the founding documents of the industrial countries' Organization for Economic Cooperation and Development (OECD). In particular, on 12 December 1961 the Council of the OECD adopted the Code of Liberalization of Capital Movements in which the member states agreed to 'progressively abolish between one another' restrictions on movements of capital 'to the extent necessary for effective economic cooperation'.[15] Although the code represented the most explicit international statement of intent regarding the discouragement of capital controls, it left significant scope for member states to make exceptions for certain types of capital transfer and to take any actions considered necessary for the 'maintenance of public order or ... the protection of essential security interests'.[16] In the event of balance of payments problems that it considered severe, a member state was also permitted by the code 'temporarily' to derogate from its liberalization obligations.[17]

For the signatory states, in short, the OECD code extended and clarified the fundamental normative consensus of Bretton Woods. But it did not change the essential rules governing international finance. Freer capital movements across borders were to be encouraged in the context of a liberal international economy. But states retained the right to impede that movement whenever they determined that conditions so warranted. During the decade following the formation of the OECD, the importance states attached to that right became evident.

In the wake of the persistent current account imbalances experienced throughout the 1960s and early 1970s, virtually all the leading industrial states resorted to various types of controls on short-term capital movements. Even the United States itself embarked upon a series of experiments designed to control disequilibrating outflows and defend the pegged exchange rate system designed at Bretton Woods.[18] Similar controls were put in place by other states in deficit, while various states in surplus adopted measures to ward off unwelcome inflows. The story of the eventual collapse of the exchange rate system is well known and not in need of recapitulation here.[19] For present purposes, however, it is important to note that as the system was collapsing, multilateral discussions on the future regulation of capital movements continued.

In 1972, in an atmosphere of crisis, an intergovernmental forum on international monetary reform was established. Labeled the Committee of Twenty of the IMF Board of Governors, its real work was undertaken by a staff drawn from the finance ministries and central banks of the leading monetary powers. Since capital mobility was a key issue of the day, the staff assigned an analytical project to a group of technical experts. The experts were essentially asked to examine the problem of speculative capital flows. Despite difficulties encountered in specifying the extent of the problem, the final report of that group conceded that disequilibrating flows could continue to disrupt even flexible exchange rate arrangements. It concluded, however, that although capital controls could not be forsworn, they should not become permanent features of a reformed system because of their potentially negative impact on trade and beneficial investment flows. In this connection the group also recommended that governments seek to craft a new code of conduct for the use of capital controls and that the code be monitored by an international agency, such as the IMF. This recommendation was not followed up.

To the frustration of reformers, for this and other reasons the final report of the Committee of Twenty did not succeed in laying the groundwork for a new monetary system.[20] In the end, all that proved politically feasible was an amendment to the Articles of Agreement of the IMF that essentially legalized floating exchange rates. Although the new Articles asserted for the first time that the exchange of capital between countries should be facilitated by the international monetary system, the rights and obligations of either member states or the IMF with regard to capital movements not directly related to trade were left unspecified.

In terms of the economic paradigm associated with the pioneering work of Robert Mundell and Marcus Fleming, the unheroic conclusion of the monetary reform exercise of the 1970s represented a collective and mainly informal decision by states to abandon one set of policy trade-offs and replace them with another. In short, during the heyday of the original Bretton Woods system, they apparently sought both foreign exchange rate stability and national monetary policy autonomy, and they were willing to tolerate limits on capital mobility in order to achieve those objectives. As that system was breaking down, they gave priority to capital mobility and monetary autonomy and were willing to abandon exchange rate stability.[21]

Following the breakdown, states collectively encouraged the expansion of international capital movements. This occurred even as some states, mainly in Europe, sought to restore a degree of exchange rate stability for themselves by limiting their own monetary autonomy within regional arrangements. Sometimes they did so through direct policy actions designed to liberate market forces, finance budget and trade deficits, or respond to competitive threats from other states. At other times they did so by not taking decisions. Having set in train a system that both lacked a reliable mechanism for pegging currency values and encouraged inward foreign direct investment, individual states subsequently found that further capital liberalization, combined with enhanced market supervision, represented the least costly policy alternative.[22] The outcome has been the widening adoption of policies aimed at capital decontrol and the integration of financial markets.

To be sure, capital flows continue to encounter 'frictions' at national borders, that is, there has yet to arise a true global financial market characterized by perfect capital mobility and structural homogeneity.[23] Still, it is clear that governmental policies formerly accommodating the possibility, even at times the necessity, of controls on short-term capital movements have lately converged in the opposite direction. Such convergent policies, and a consequent reorientation of the expectations of state and market actors, suggest a fundamental break with the original Bretton Woods rules. In 1989 that convergence was recognized by the member countries of the OECD as they widened the scope of the Capital Movements Code. Although escape clauses were retained, the subsequent activism of the OECD in working to minimize the reservations of member states suggests an attempt to replace the formal legal right to control capital movements with a new rule.

THE LANGUAGE OF INTERNATIONAL CAPITAL MOBILITY

Walter Wriston, a former chairman of Citibank, described and defended the process of capital decontrol as follows:

> The gold standard [of the nineteenth century], replaced by the gold exchange standard, which was replaced by the Bretton Woods arrangements, has now been replaced by the information standard. Unlike the other standards, the information standard is in place, operating, will never go away, and has substantially changed the world. What it means, very simply, is that bad monetary and fiscal policies anywhere in the world are reflected within minutes on the Reuters screens in the trading rooms of the world. Money only goes where it's wanted, and only stays where it's well treated, and once you tie the world together with telecommunications and information, the ball game is over. It's a new world, and the fact is, the information standard is more draconian than any gold standard ... For the first time in history, the politicians of the world can't stop it. It's beyond the political control of the world, and that's the good news.[24]

Despite the exaggerated liberalism of this language, Wriston rightly suggests that the norm of cross-national capital mobility gradually achieved priority over other economic policy goals in the 1970s. This ascendancy, however, generated significant strains in various domestic and international political arenas. Export-intensive economies with relatively rigid labor markets, for example Germany, found the consequent volatility of exchange rates increasingly disruptive. At the same time, a lack of effective coordination in the supervision of intermediaries operating across national borders contributed to a series of financial disasters. In reaction, during the 1980s movements towards European monetary integration and expanded international concertation on financial market supervision accelerated. Neither movement, however, ultimately compromised the new priority of the capital mobility norm. Even the developing country debt crisis, which dominated the financial policy agenda during that decade, affected the distribution of international capital more than its mobility in

principle, which was greatly enhanced by the now-rapid development of new financial technologies. In Wriston's words,
'technology has combined with finance in a new and unique
way that makes obsolete some of the old ideas of compartmen-
talized national markets'. Robert Slighton, a senior official
from Chase Manhattan Bank, puts the matter more simply:
'There is a global capital market, period'.[25]

Nevertheless, global financial integration and the fact that
citizens continue to hold their national governments responsible for national economic performance has created an ever
more generally perceived tension. On the one hand, in a
more complex financial environment they seek the jobs, investment, new technology and prestige that mobile capital,
whether embodied in short-term financial flows or long-term
fixed investments, appears to promise. On the other hand
those same governments must craft domestic economic
ground rules that strike their own internal balance between
competitive efficiency and other social values. In many cases
these include fairness, equality of opportunity and geographic
equity. Moreover democratic national governments must
strike that balance in societies that will not easily abide the
notion that all choices related to a basic factor of production
are unalterably constrained, especially when the earlier decisions of governments themselves created that constraint.

The resulting dilemma for government policy makers is not
new. It is no coincidence that obfuscation turns out to be
politically useful. The news media assist with headlines like:
'Governments Lose Clout in New Monetary Order'. And
financial commentators can always be counted on to say things
like 'the privilege of government is being squeezed away' by
global financial markets.[26]

One obvious problem with this language is that only states
can establish and secure the property rights upon which those
markets are based, and only they can ensure the requisite
modicum of market stability.[27] Directly or indirectly, states continue to meet that challenge, even as they seek to exploit the
efficiency gains promised by increasing financial integration.
The fact that individual states have limited abilities fully to
meet resulting obligations explains why all have been impelled
in recent years to cooperate more extensively with one another
on the supervisory front.[28] But measures to deal with what

financiers call 'systemic risk' – the risk that failure in one financial market will spread – imply an irreducible kind of state guarantee. Like all guarantees, those that underpin international capital markets have actual as well as potential costs. These must be borne by someone.

Open capital markets and the expanding availability of multinational options work to ensure that the most mobile, creditworthy and externally oriented firms, sectors and factors of production avoid the full impact of such costs. In the absence of countervailing action, the least mobile firms, sectors and factors necessarily bear most of the burdens created as governments respond to pressures for financial guarantees. The intensity of consequent social and political tensions and the responses of states appear to vary across countries and across business cycles.[29] Nevertheless this leaves the world with a problem akin to those Inis Claude once termed problems of 'collective legitimization'. The norm of international capital mobility, quite simply, lacks 'formally declared and generally acknowledged legitimacy'.[30] As distinct from the issue of trade in goods and services, national legislatures and multilateral institutions have not clarified the character of rights, compensatory obligations or avenues for redress associated with the freedom of capital flows.

THE CHALLENGE OF MULTILATERAL ECONOMIC MANAGEMENT

Corporate financiers, as well as spokesmen for national governments, which are themselves among the largest borrowers of international capital, use the language of capital mobility to obscure the notion that other choices have been possible. It is the language of what Karl Polanyi caricatured as 'the self-regulating market'.[31] In its most profound sense, it is an antipolitical language that seeks to rationalize the disruption of traditional economic and social structures. Polanyi's fellow Austrian, Joseph Schumpeter, famously described that process as one of 'creative destruction'.[32] As Polanyi pointed out, however, and as Schumpeter feared, civil societies, even if reshaped by new economic forces, find ways to defend themselves from 'self-regulating' markets. It seems, nevertheless, that those defenses are seldom perfected before markets aspiring to such a condition self-destruct.

Where might we look to observe such defensive impulses today? Firstly, we might look to the sources of rising trade protectionism in a number of countries and regions around the world. In this regard the debate between Keynes and White is still alive as states find themselves hard-pressed to reconcile free trade and free capital movements. Secondly, we might look at the agendas of proliferating populist and nationalist political movements. Although the issue is less politically salient than labor mobility, when demagogues in Europe ranging across a wide spectrum from LePen in France to Zhirinovsky in Russia broach the idea of limiting the influence of international (or German or American or Jewish) capital, they strike a chord with deep historical resonances. When Ross Perot alluded to the growing power of Japanese capital in the United States during the 1980s, he struck a similar chord. The extreme caution evident in much of East Asia on the issue of Western-style financial deregulation seems grounded in a parallel sense of unease. To the extent that capital flows are perceived to create or sustain relationships of dominance and subservience, policies of financial liberalization are obvious targets for political leaders promising their followers, in a word, autonomy.

International capital mobility disrupts long-standing patterns of life. It is unleashed by political forces and its effects are intrinsically political. For an increasing number of states today, it appears to represent a key element in the least costly of possible alternative economic strategies. Few, however, are directly addressing its unintended consequences. These include, most importantly, the building up of resentment among those not benefiting in the near term. Here is the core of what was described above as a problem of legitimacy. As is especially obvious in countries attempting to make the 'transition' to democracy, such resentment can clearly sow the seeds for a backlash if capital mobility does not reliably and expeditiously help to bring widespread prosperity. Similar misgivings are not inconceivable in advanced countries, especially if capital mobility and exchange rate instability interact in such a way as to exacerbate concerns about future economic and social well-being.

In the world's strongest civil societies, however, it is now likely that it would take a serious crisis to shift dominant internal perceptions of the respective costs and benefits of capital decontrol. But crises happen. Analysts should be cautious, therefore, about interpreting the current dimensions of international capital mobility as constitutive of a truly exogenous structure that irrevocably binds those societies and their states. A *collective* movement away from capital decontrol may be undesirable, but it remains entirely possible.[33] If it were not, then why would the world's most sophisticated financiers, central bankers and finance ministers fly into paroxysms of anxiety whenever a major financial institution gets into trouble, whenever the world's stock markets fall precipitously or whenever a major borrower threatens to default? To those charged with securing them, the disintegration of international capital markets remains all-too imaginable. It is from that conundrum that international political economists might usefully take their bearings for future research on the normative underpinnings of those markets.

Going back to the Mundell–Fleming framework, if national governments are to take seriously the concerns that are increasingly being expressed about exchange rate instability, even in mainstream policy circles,[34] and if they want to preserve whatever efficiency benefits international capital mobility provides, then it would seem that they have to begin reconsidering the priority they assign to monetary autonomy. Indeed some smaller countries have moved to address such concerns by voluntarily – but rarely irrevocably – giving up exchange rate flexibility. For the major economic powers whose autonomy will never really seep away through some kind of automatic economic process, it might one day be timely to consider a similar compromise.

The Group of Seven has in recent years paid obeisance to this logic. When difficult choices need to be made, however, the three largest members of the group recapitulate the choices of 1973, and the language of international capital mobility provides cover. For the big three – the United States, Germany and Japan – the essential trade-off remains capital mobility and exchange rate flexibility in return for the maximum feasible degree of autonomy in monetary policy. In France the choice was made in 1983 deliberately to limit autonomy by not abandoning a linkage between the franc and the mark. For Britain and Canada, the path of least resistance has led to a less desirable outcome – capital mobility, exchange rate instability and little real autonomy in monetary policy.[35]

Under what conditions do powerful and potentially dominant states voluntarily relinquish policy autonomy? This remains the key question for future research in this area. The question is usually put more diplomatically or rephrased as an anodyne assertion. As Paul Volcker's 'Bretton Woods Commission' recently put it: domestic macroeconomic policy can no longer be formulated in isolation.[36] But of course it can be formulated in relative isolation, at least in the United States, Japan and Germany. And international capital mobility is a necessary condition. If a current account deficit is the consequence, open international capital markets will finance it. If a surplus results, those same markets provide the necessary financial outlet. Through them the rest of the world helps to bear the resulting economic and political burdens. Once again the language of international capital mobility, with its overtones of inevitability, provides a useful resource for dissimulation.

In the real world, and in 'normal' times, the policy autonomy of a dominant state is probably only compromised by its own willingness to embrace exchange rate stability as a higher priority. In the contemporary environment this, in turn, would entail a willingness both to act as a reliable monetary anchor for other states and to address internal distributional questions. When power is diffuse in the international system – that is, when there is no single dominant state, or when the power of a particular social class is spread widely across diverse societies – the question is whether this path towards legitimacy and stability is ultimately blocked. Another way to ask such a question is whether multilateral systemic management by responsible governments is truly feasible. The answer is neither obvious nor inevitable.

Notes

*   Support for this essay came from the Social Sciences and Humanities Research Council of Canada (grant 410–91–1308). A previous version

was published as 'Capital Mobility, State Autonomy, and Political Legitimacy', *Journal of International Affairs*, vol. 48, no. 2 (Winter 1995), pp. 369–88. Portions of this chapter are published by permission of the *Journal of International Affairs* and the Trustees of Columbia University in the City of New York.

1. For example, in addition to references cited below, see S. Strange, *Casino Capitalism* (Oxford: Basil Blackwell, 1986); B. Cohen, *In Whose Interest? International Banking and American Foreign Policy* (New Haven, Conn.: Yale University Press, 1986); J. Hawley, *Dollars and Borders* (New York: M. E. Sharpe, 1987); R. Bryant, *International Financial Intermediation* (Washington, DC: Brookings, 1987); L. W. Pauly, *Opening Financial Markets* (Ithaca, NY: Cornell University Press, 1988); A. Walter, *World Power and World Money* (London: Harvester Wheatsheaf, 1991); G. Underhill, 'Markets Beyond Politics? The State and the Internationalization of Financial Markets', *European Journal of Political Research*, vol. 19 (1991), pp. 197–255; T. Porter, *States, Markets and Regimes in Global Finance* (New York: St Martin's, 1993); and P. Cerny (ed.), *Finance and World Politics* (Aldershot, UK: Edward Elgar, 1993).

2. An outstanding example, upon which I have relied in this chapter, is E. Helleiner, *States and the Reemergence of Global Finance* (Ithaca, NY: Cornell University Press, 1994).

3. For example S. Maxfield, *Governing Capital* (Ithaca, NY: Cornell University Press, 1990); M. C. Webb, 'International Structures, Government Interests, and International Coordination of Macroeconomic Adjustment Policies', *International Organization*, vol. 45 (1991), pp. 309–42; M. Loriaux, *France After Hegemony* (Ithaca, NY: Cornell University Press, 1991); J. B. Goodman and L. W. Pauly, 'The Obsolescence of Capital Controls? Economic Management in an Age of Global Markets', *World Politics*, vol. 46, no. 1 (1993), pp. 50–82; P. Kurzer, *Business and Banking* (Ithaca, NY: Cornell University Press, 1993); S. Strange, *States and Markets*, 2nd edn (New York: Basil Blackwell, 1994); and D. M. Andrews, 'Capital Mobility and State Autonomy: Toward a Structural Theory of International Monetary Relations', *International Studies Quarterly*, vol. 38 (1994), pp. 193–218.

4. I am using the term 'antipolitical' in a manner consistent with the polarity well-described by C. Lindblom in *Politics and Markets* (New York: Basic Books, 1977).

5. J. G. Ruggie, 'International Regimes, Transactions, and Change: Embedded Liberalism in the Postwar Economic Order', *International Organization*, vol. 36, no. 2 (1982).

6. Even Margaret Thatcher's Herculean efforts to change those expectations in Britain did little to undermine the actual scale and scope of the British welfare state.

7. On the former, work directly relevant to international systemic questions extends from the classic statement of F. H. Hinsley in *Sovereignty* (New York: Basic Books, 1966) to recent perspectives offered, for example, by J. G. Ruggie in 'Territoriality and Beyond: Problematizing Modernity in International Relations', *International Organization*,

vol. 47, no. 1 (1994), pp. 139–74; S. Barkin and B. Cronin in 'The State and the Nation: Changing Norms and the Rules of Sovereignty in International Relations', *International Organization*, vol. 48, no. 1 (1994) pp. 107–30; and A. Wendt in 'Collective Identity Formation and the International State', *American Political Science Review*, vol. 88, no. 2 (1994), pp. 384–96. On the latter, a clear line of relevant debate links R. Keohane and J. Nye (eds), *Transnational Relations and World Politics* (Cambridge, Mass.: Harvard University Press, 1972) to such works as P. J. Katzenstein (ed.), *Between Power and Plenty* (Madison, Wis.: University of Wisconsin Press, 1978); S. D. Krasner (ed.), *International Regimes* (Ithaca, NY: Cornell University Press, 1983); D. Baldwin (ed.), *Neorealism and Neoliberalism: The Contemporary Debate* (New York: Columbia University Press, 1993); and R. Putnam *et al.* (eds), *Double-Edged Diplomacy* (Berkeley, Cal.: University of California Press, 1993).

8.   On the importance of this difference, see C. R. Henning, *Currencies and Politics in the United States, Germany, and Japan* (Washington, DC: Institute for International Economics, 1994).

9.   The test is whether the right to exercise effective political authority is matched by the perception of an obligation to comply. Thomas Franck persuasively adapted this Weberian conception of legitimacy to the international sphere by defining it as the 'quality of a rule which derives from a perception on the part of those to whom it is addressed that it has come into being in accordance with right process'. As indicators for the rightness of a process and the legitimacy of resulting rules, he proposes tests of determinacy, symbolic validation, coherence and adherence to a normative hierarchy. The capital mobility regime would fall short on all counts. See T. Franck 'Legitimacy in the International System', *American Journal of International Law*, vol. 82 (1988), pp. 705–59.

10.   This section draws in part on my contribution (chapter 6) to U.S. Congress, Office of Technology Assessment, *Multinationals and the National Interest: Playing By Different Rules* (Washington, DC: U.S. Government Printing Office, 1993); further references can be found there.

11.   J. M. Keynes, 'National self-sufficiency', *Yale Review*, vol. 21, no. 4 (1933).

12.   The view that all capital controls should be discouraged later became even more prominent in the American position, a development many students of the subject have attributed mainly to the resurgent influence of the New York financial community after the war ended. See M. de Cecco, 'Origins of the Postwar Payments System', *Cambridge Journal of Economics*, vol. 3 (1979), pp. 49–61. That influence was evidently not strong enough during the 1960s, however, to prevent the American government itself from experimenting with capital controls when the need arose.

13.   See Article VI, sections 1 and 3 of the Articles of Agreement of the International Monetary Fund. For his part, Keynes interpreted this compromise as follows: 'Not merely as a feature of the transition, but

as a permanent arrangement, the plan accords to every member Government the explicit right to control all capital movements. What used to be heresy is now endorsed as orthodox ... It follows that our right to control the domestic capital market is secured on firmer foundations than ever before, and is formally accepted as a proper part of agreed international arrangements'. Quoted in J. Gold, 'International Capital Movements Under the Law of the International Monetary Fund', *Pamphlet Series*, no. 21 (Washington, DC: IMF, 1977), p. 11.

14. To take one example, note that leads and lags in current payments can effectively create 'capital flows' which may or may not be equilibrating for a country's overall external balance. Controls on such flows have typically included a broad range of explicit restrictions, special taxes or tacit arrangements designed essentially to discourage certain kinds of financial transfers between residents and non-residents. See OECD, *Controls on International Capital Movements* (Paris: OECD, 1982).

15. OECD, *Code of Liberalization of Capital Movements* (Paris: OECD, October 1986) Article 1. Also see OECD, *Introduction to the OECD Codes of Liberalization* (Paris: OECD, 1987). Furthermore, the signatories agreed to 'endeavor to extend the measures of liberalization to all members of the International Monetary Fund'.

16. OECD Code, op. cit., Article 3.

17. Ibid., Article 7.

18. On the US resort to controls, see J. Conybeare, *U.S. Foreign Economic Policy and the International Capital Markets* (New York: Garland, 1988).

19. See B. J. Cohen, *Organizing the World's Money* (New York: Basic, 1977); F. L. Block, *The Origins of International Economic Disorder* (Berkeley: University of California Press, 1977); J. S. Odell, *U.S. International Monetary Policy* (Princeton: Princeton University Press, 1982); and J. Gowa, *Closing and Gold Window* (Ithaca, NY: Cornell University Press, 1983).

20. See J. Williamson, *The Failure of World Monetary Reform, 1971–1974* (New York: New York University Press, 1977).

21. For background, see R. Mundell, 'The Monetary Dynamics of International Adjustment under Fixed and Floating Exchange Rates', *Quarterly Journal of Economics*, vol. 74 (May 1960); M. Fleming, 'Domestic Financial Policies under Fixed and Floating Exchange Rates', *IMF Staff Papers*, no. 9 (1962); and R. Mundell, 'Capital Mobility and Stabilization Policy under Fixed and Flexible Exchange Rates', *Canadian Journal of Economics and Political Science*, vol. 29 (November 1963), pp. 475–85. Note that the original Mundell–Fleming analysis did not give sufficient weight to the link between exchange rates and domestic prices. In practice that link assures that under normal circumstances only the largest economies least dependent on international trade and investment could aspire to a high degree of monetary autonomy. See R. Cooper, *The Economics of Interdependence* (New York: McGraw-Hill, 1968); B. J. Cohen, 'The Triad and the Unholy Trinity: Lessons for the Pacific Region', in R. Higgot *et al.* (eds), *Pacific Economic Relations in the 1990s* (London:

Allen & Unwin, 1993); and T. Padoa-Schioppa, 'The European Monetary System: A Long-Term View', in F. Giavazzi *et al.*, *The European Monetary System* (Cambridge, Mass.: Cambridge University Press, 1987).

22. For an expansion of this point, see Goodman and Pauly, op. cit.

23. See J. A. Frankel, 'Measuring International Capital Mobility: A Review', *American Economic Review*, vol. 82, no. 2 (1992), pp. 197–202.

24. Quoted in J. A. Frieden, *Banking on the World: The Politics of International Finance* (New York: Basil Blackwell, 1987), pp. 114–15.

25. Ibid., p. 164.

26. *International Herald Tribune*, 7 July 1994, p. 1. For analysis along this line, see R. O'Brien, *Global Financial Integration: The End of Geography* (London: Pinter, 1992).

27. The point is well-made in J. E. Thomson and S. D. Krasner, 'Global Transactions and the Consolidation of Sovereignty', in E. O. Czempiel and J. N. Rosenau (eds), *Global Changes and Theoretical Challenges* (Lexington, Mass.: D. C. Heath, 1989), pp. 195–219. See also R. Gilpin, *The Political Economy of International Relations* (Princeton: Princeton University Press, 1986), chap. 8.

28. See E. Kapstein, *Governing Global Finance* (Cambridge, Mass.: Harvard University Press, 1994); J. Goodman, *Monetary Sovereignty* (Ithaca, NY: Cornell University Press, 1992). This is an important part of the logic that appears currently to be driving policy planning on capital movements and monetary integration within the European Union.

29. For relevant research, much of which is grounded in the politics of trade, see H. Milner, *Resisting Protectionism* (Princeton, NJ: Princeton University Press, 1989); R. Rogowski, *Commerce and Coalitions* (Princeton, NJ: Princeton University Press, 1989); J. A. Frieden, 'Invested interests: the politics of national economic policies in a world of global finance', *International Organization*, vol. 45, no. 4 (Autumn 1991), pp. 425–51; J. A. Frieden, *Debt, Development, and Democracy* (Princeton, NJ: Princeton University Press, 1991); C. Schonhardt-Bailey, 'Specific factors, Capital Markets, Portfolio Diversification, and Free Trade: Domestic Determinants of the Repeal of the Corn Laws', *World Politics*, vol. 43 (1991), pp. 545–69; and J. A. Winters, 'Power and the Control of Capital', *World Politics*, vol. 46, no. 3 (1994), pp. 419–52.

30. I. L. Claude, Jr, 'Collective Legitimization as a Political Function of the United Nations', *International Organization*, vol. 20 (1966), pp. 267–79. On the more general problem of legitimation in advanced capitalism, see J. Habermas, *Legitimation Crisis* (Boston: Beacon Press, 1975); and R. Cox, *Production, Power and World Order* (New York: Columbia University Press, 1987).

31. K. Polanyi, *The Great Transformation* (Boston: Beacon Press, 1957).

32. J. Schumpeter, *Capitalism, Socialism, and Democracy* (New York: Harper & Row, 1950).

33. On the feasibility of a reversion amidst the turmoil of the 1970s, see Helleiner, op. cit., p. 118. The theme continues to recur in official documents. It is rehearsed, for example, in a study on international

capital movements commissioned by the ministers and governors of the Group of Ten in the wake of the September 1992 crisis in the European Monetary System. See *IMF Survey*, 17 May 1993, p. 148.

34. See, for example, P. Volcker and T. Gyohten, *Changing Fortunes* (New York: Times Books, 1992); Bretton Woods Commission, *Bretton Woods: Looking to the Future* (Washington, DC: Bretton Woods Commission, 1994); C. F. Bergsten (ed.) *Conference on the Future of the Bretton Woods Systems* (Washington, DC: Institute for International Economics, 1994).

35. The erosion of autonomy in these countries is in substantial part a function of feedback effects between exchange rates and domestic prices. In the Canadian case the problem is significantly exacerbated by a relatively high dependence on external sources to finance overall government indebtedness.

36. *IMF Survey*, 8 August 1994, p. 249.

8 Politics in Retreat: Redrawing Our Political Maps*

Norbert Lechner

THE EROSION OF POLITICAL MAPS

In Latin America, as in other regions, a sort of antipolitics is gaining influence and even political power (Collor, Fujimori, Menem) which, without openly questioning democracy, is profoundly altering its exercise. These new, antipolitical phenomena represent more than simple 'deviant cases'; they form part of a more general process of redefinition and restructuring. We are witnessing not only political changes, but a change in politics itself.

The situation in Latin America forces us to revise two tactical premises which have been implicit in the processes of democratic transition. Our defense of politics in opposition to authoritarian antipolitics had implicitly identified politics with democratic politics. Yet as soon as the 'business' of politics re-emerged, its democratic character faded away. Thus we must again ask ourselves an ancient question: what is the meaning of democratic politics? That question compels us to reconsider yet another premise. Early in the transitions from authoritarian rule we took for granted that democracy would be our point of arrival. However as we moved ahead with this process we believed was leading us to democracy, our goal shifted like a *fata morgana*. We discovered that the journey of democratization does not lead to an unequivocal destiny, fixed once and for all.

There is a deep uneasiness with modernity as we usually understand it: as the normative reflexivity and the political steering of societal processes. The impression prevails that contemporary processes of transformation escape our control. Overshadowed by the antinomy between democracy and

168

authoritarianism, the tension between modernity and modernization has been ignored for many years.

The struggle against authoritarianism served to revalue democratic regimes, but at the same time it dried up all reflections on political dynamics. We have forgotten that democracy is an historic movement whose meaning we must bring up to date with changing circumstances. It is true that any epoch is tempted to view itself as an exceptional period, and thus as the end of history. But later on contexts change and things are read differently – not because new 'truths' appear but because reality itself changes.

I wonder if the new panorama does not also change our very way of looking at politics. We find ourselves in the midst of a diffuse struggle which is still at the larval stage with regard to how we understand democracy and democratic politics. Such political conflict should not astonish us. It is part of all major transformations which modify the institutionalized forms of conducting and of conceiving politics. In fact our malaise with politics can be explained neither by an economic crisis nor by a political one. The economic hardship of Latin American countries, which is rooted in foreign debt and structural adjustment measures as well as in the enormous social costs stemming from them, is notorious. Nevertheless there exists a broad-based agreement both on the need for such economic reforms and on the urgency to reduce social inequalities. We are not facing a political crisis in the usual sense in which ideological polarization and partisan mobilization generate conflicts that overwhelm democratic institutions. On the contrary it seems to me that this discomfort is not so much related to economic and political–institutional problems as to a new 'cultural climate'.

The relationship between politics and culture is not the only significant element for understanding democracy. In fact it is not even a matter of high priority. But it allows us to visualize the fact that the current uneasiness with democratic politics is crystallizing into a new perspective. The usual images of politics, and therefore traditional expectations with regard to political action, are more and more difficult to replicate under the new conditions. They are maintained by inertia while we seek to form another idea of politics and democracy, which is more concordant with everyday experience.

If we further reflect on this intuition we arrive at the basic
parameters according to which we preconceive politics. The
new context alters the dynamics of political institutions and
actors. Yet it seems to me that, beyond those political changes
in a narrow sense, one of the greatest challenges for Latin
American democracies lies in the area of political culture. This
encompasses not only beliefs and preferences gathered in
public opinion surveys, but also symbolic representations
and collective imaginations – in other words, those bits of
'evidence' people do not make explicit because they consider
them 'normal' and 'natural'. It is in this cultural sphere that
we form our images of politics as well as our prejudices about
societal problems and their possible solutions.

A 'culturalist' approach is usually thought to be more problematic and controversial than other approaches. One recent
example is the interpretation offered by Charles Maier, who
deciphers the current discontent with democracy as a moral
crisis.[1] It is easy to agree with the cautious and subtle way he
describes the symptoms: a sudden sensation of being dis-
connected from history, the disaffection with the *nomenklatura*
of any ideological sign, and a recurrent skepticism towards the
doctrines of social progress. Even though I share his intention,
I nevertheless fear that the notion of a 'moral crisis' may lead
us not to a renovation of ethical–normative principles but to
an explosion of irrational attitudes. When the usual guidance
criteria fail and tensions become unbearable, returning to the
moral trenches appears attractive; it substitutes simple and
pure convictions for the complex process of developing and
selecting alternatives. History has taught us too many times
the unfortunate consequences of pretending to save morality
by denying evil. In order to avoid any confusion of politics
with the salvation of souls (Max Weber), I prefer to use the
well-known metaphor of the map.

At the present, political processes resemble a journey
without a compass. Since democratic politics lacks a preestablished objective, the traveler needs maps which order
reality and offer orientation. The metaphor of a map refers to
the coordinates of space and time which we use to represent
social reality. Maps help us to delimit space, establish hierar-
chies and priorities, structure boundaries and distances, determine goals and design strategies. In essence, maps help us to

visualize things in their proper proportions. The maps we are using, however, have become obsolete and disproportionate. Things are no longer where they used to be, and the scales have changed. And the more details we add to these outdated maps the worse things get, because the only thing we achieve is to create false confidence. It is better to realize that we are living not only through a crisis of ideological maps, but also through an erosion of cognitive maps. We have to revise our political cartography.

The crisis of ideological maps is evident everywhere. After the excessive ideological polarization of the 1960s and 1970s, we have welcomed the decline of ideology as a sign of realism. Instead of subjecting reality to a prefabricated scheme, social complexity is accepted. In the absence of interpretative clues, however, this complexity turns out to be unintelligible. We now discover the relevance of ideologies as maps for reducing the complexity of social reality. Indeed the antagonism between capitalism and socialism has given rise to simplistic interpretations and ill-fated dichotomies, but it has operated as an effective scheme for structuring political positions and conflicts throughout this century. The fall of the Berlin Wall (to use a symbolic point of reference) brought about the collapse of this scheme, and with it a whole set of milestones vanished, a whole set of focal points for political classification and for the structuring of reality. Thus, in the absence of all the customary points of reference a familiar landscape offered, politics is perceived as disorder.

To my understanding, politics in its modern conception aims at the deliberate construction of a societal order. Once divine principles and ancestral traditions are lost, politics takes their place as the privileged authority for bringing order into social life. In modern, secular societies, where nothing is fixed or predetermined, politics is expected to establish and to assure 'law and order', and not only in legal terms. In a more fundamental sense, politics is also called upon to guarantee the moral and cultural ordering of communal life, to create a framework of reference shared by citizens in all their plurality.

The difficulty of fulfilling this task can be observed with particular clarity in political parties. Their main job is to offer interpretive schemes and practical options which allow citizens to order their values, their preferences and their fears, and to

integrate them into collective identities. Because of the profound transformations worldwide, parties and party systems
are no longer able to develop such keys of orientation, and
the temptation arises to impose some kind of 'national unity'
through populist or plebiscitarian invocations. In fact, feeling
dispersed and unprotected, people long for the absolute certainties and immutable identities of the past. In this context
we can understand the current disenchantment with politics
and the citizenry's lack of identification with parties not as
opposition to democracy, not even as a rejection of the parties,
but simply as the result of a distressing absence of interpretive
codes.

We can observe a deeper cultural transformation which is
underlying this ideological crisis. A restructuring of our cognitive maps is underway, that is, a restructuring of the mental
coordinates and interpretative codes through which we make
social processes intelligible. This is perhaps one of the most
significant features of our time, the erosion of shared interpretative codes. The contested meaning of democracy is an
illustrative example. The lack of intelligibility reinforces a
climate of uncertainty which cannot be resolved through more
information. In politics as in economics, accumulating data
only increases the weight of the unknown. Uncertainty can
only be absorbed through intersubjective links which allow us
to tame the vicissitudes of the future.

THE SPATIAL TRANSFORMATION OF POLITICS

The processes of globalization and segmentation that charac-
terize our times are accompanied by a profound restructuring
of the political realm. In the first place, the scales of politics
are changing. Dimensions, proportions and measures are
becoming altered and politics, as a consequence, displaced
and dislocated. The former congruence between the political,
economic and cultural realms delimited by national boundaries is dissolving. Economic, cultural and administrative
processes are being integrated on a supranational level, while
the integration of citizens barely reaches the national level. We
have all seen how internationalization redefines the actors
involved in politics, the political agenda, and even the institu-

tional framework of politics. The recent free trade agreements (Mercosur, NAFTA) limit the latitude and the political options available to the respective countries. This has stabilizing effects, but also adverse ones. The sphere of popular sovereignty, and hence that of citizenship, becomes vague. Issues of major social impact are removed from the public agenda while others of scant relevance are magnified. This lack of proportion creates doubts about what can be expected from politics. It becomes impossible to determine the value of politics.

Another aspect worth highlighting is the phenomenon of shifting boundaries. On the one side, boundaries become more tenuous and porous. The massive flows of migration, the rapid circulation of cultural moods and the relative uniformity of consumption habits all break down old barriers. However these new commonalties, expanded almost compulsively, do not mean that we share a common culture. Therefore, on the other side, some boundaries become more rigid and controversial. Collective identities are always based on distinctions from others, and today differences are more rapidly drawn and also more easily perceived as threatening aggression. This triggers fears of conflict and provokes a strong desire for stability. In this situation of diffuse and shifting boundaries, politics faces obvious difficulties in expressing, connecting and ordering the existing universe of unstable, overlapping or antagonistic identities.

Changing distances also contribute to the destructuring of the political realm. On the one hand, the extension of transnational circuits to very diverse spheres reduces distances. The international integration of political systems has increased considerably during the past years, even though the mechanisms of political regulation are weaker than in other spheres and often inoperative. We need only to recall the new roles played by the United Nations, the Organization of American States and the Group of Rio. Interaction has increased and bonds have multiplied, which, for better or worse, restricts the field of political action and generates continuity. On the other hand, however, internationalization has given birth to processes of segmentation that widen distances within each society. Thus socioeconomic inequalities intensify and political distances increase, although in a different way than in previous cases of ideological polarization. Initiatives for decentralization weaken the links between national and local elites while, in general, old clientelistic networks successfully adapt to the new environment. Gaining predominance are new mediating mechanisms (such as television) that generate rapid and immediate yet volatile bonds since they are based on shared emotions as opposed to shared interests.

The different elements just mentioned allow us to visualize the spatial restructuring of politics. They are too contradictory, however, to pin down the direction of these changes or to circumscribe the emergent space with any precision. I propose, therefore, that we proceed by approaching two basic points of reference in the new context: the expansion of the market and the redimensioning of the state.

Modernity has brought about the transition from a natural, given order to an artificial, produced one, and it has enthroned politics as the sphere responsible for organizing social life. Yet in recent times this idea of politics has been questioned in the name of self-regulation. As during the era of Polanyi's Great Transformation,[2] the 'laws of the market' are once again seen as representing the constitutive principle of social organization. In recent years the attempt to substitute politics with the market as the privileged means for regulation and coordination has undoubtedly found its maximum expression in neoliberalism. Nowadays it is easier to discern two aspects that have been frequently confused in the generic use of the term. On the one hand neoliberalism promises the affluence of market societies and hints at the fact that our countries have no choice other than to adapt their economic structures to the new modalities of the world market. On the other hand Latin American experiences disprove a core assumption of neoliberalism. The market on its own neither generates nor sustains social order. Structural adjustment programs that ignore political–institutional consensus building reinforce the disarticulation of society. The high levels of poverty and social inequality represent only the most dramatic expression of the disintegrative force of free markets. Even the international financial agencies have modified their previous positions. They now assign high priority to political factors as key factors for the viability of economic programs.[3] And still the political reconstruction of society encounters enormous difficulties.

Due to the very violence with which market mechanisms have been imposed in Latin America, they have acquired a momentum of their own which is difficult to regulate. One of the new market societies' most notorious features is the expansion of the market to non-economic spheres. In particular, the political field is literally taken over, even if the consequences are not in line with the idea of a self-regulating society. On the contrary, the uncontrollable advancement of a capitalist market economy tends to subvert the public order. Instead of giving citizens greater freedom to choose and instead of making political decisions more transparent, the enthronement of market rationality basically consecrates commercial criteria – money as the general means of exchange – to the detriment of the traditional ethos of politics as public service. This alters the communicative structure of democracy. Deliberation and debate are replaced with the exchange of goods and favors, and political negotiation increasingly resembles trade and business practices.

The imprint that market society leaves on politics should not lead us to demonize the market, whose advances, after all, are based on a transformation of the state. In fact, underneath the rhetorical surface of urgent calls for state reform, its reorganization is already underway, and little attention has been paid to its implications.

Critics from the left who oppose the state's authoritarian face and critics on the right who reject its intervention into social and economic affairs find common antistatist ground. They jointly create an antistate atmosphere in which the state is viewed as nothing more than a necessary evil. In Latin America we have gone from one extreme to another – from state idolatry to contemptuous antistatism that ignores the very nature of the state. In fact the role of the state continues to be one of the most controversial issues.

Rescaling the state's productive activity, the administrative structure, and even public services has been inevitable. It has represented a step of adjustment to changed conditions, which we may welcome to the degree that it promotes social creativity. Nevertheless any modernization of the state apparatus will produce ill-fated results if the state's symbolic significance is ignored. It will lead to situations of 'modernization without modernity'. The current discussion often overlooks the role the state plays in shaping public morality, the universe of symbols and the so-called national culture. As the state codifies linguistic and legal norms and homogenizes bureaucratic procedures and socialization in schools, it guarantees common forms of perception and reasoning as well as shared milestones of memory and hope – in other words, that common sense through which people communicate. The state embodies the symbolic unity of social coexistence without which society would not be able to recognize itself as such, that is, as a collective order.

The de facto redefinition of the state currently underway contains the risk of oversimplification. We may look, for example, at privatization policies in Latin America. Even if we accept their economic soundness in numerous cases (while others are difficult to assess in the medium and long term), there is no doubt that a strategy of massive and indiscriminate privatization undermines the institutional order. I am referring to structural changes in the relationship between the public and the private, and more specifically to transformations of the public sphere. The predominant approach dissolves the notion of 'public goods' by reducing its attention to economic competitiveness and efficiency. An 'open market' not only implies that access is restricted for many. More importantly it means that commonalties, spheres of shared interest, are diluted. Hence feelings of community lose their content. They become empty shells. Even social policies, which after all aim at compensating for the increasing social inequalities, employ strategies which focus on target groups without any reference to overarching collective identities.

In this way economic privatization generates a privatization of behavior. New ways of life based on individualist strategies emerge. They are rational and creative in adapting to competitive relationships and in taking advantage of market opportunities. But they do not assume collective commitments. On the contrary, they weaken the public sphere and hence the shared experiences, the affective bonds and the practical knowledge upon which any institutional order rests. As a consequence the new social relationships, as successful as they may be on an individual basis, increase uncertainty as well as the perception of risk and threat. Against this backdrop the recent social explosions in the region are not so much an expression of prevailing misery. Rather they represent a demand for public spheres of collective self-recognition.

The experiences just described make it necessary carefully to review fashionable propositions for strengthening civil society. No matter how relevant civil society may be, I believe it is important to emphasize the fact that civil society by itself, without reference to the state, does not generate societal order. Unilateral approaches risk ending up as leftist versions of market apologies.

Neither the strength of market society nor the downsizing of the state represent factors external to political dynamics. On the contrary, politics actually contributes to the limitation of its own sphere. This self-restraint of the political realm is likely to be a decisive experience for people. And perhaps it makes it easier to understand their loss of confidence in politics as a means of regulation and direction as well as their symmetrical trust in the decentralized coordination of private individuals, that is, in the market.

THE TEMPORAL TRANSFORMATION OF POLITICS

Maps not only represent reality. They also provide orientation. Tourists may use maps as 'travel guides'. This brings us to the notion of time. In order to approach the temporal dimension of politics I believe it is fruitful to consider two points of tension.

First, political time moves between the poles of change and continuity. In our modern, future-oriented societies, politics is in charge of constructing the future. It represents the instrument citizens dispose of in order to create the future instead of falling victim to it. Modern politics is not only action; it is also innovation. Since building the future means building something new, it values social change more than the *status quo*, renovation more than conservation. At the same time, however, politics must create continuity. It is only through their endurance that institutions may acquire moral force, a normative foundation. Citizens expect politics to be solid and consistent, regardless of being grounded on fragile relationships such as trust. Faced with the ancestral trauma of chaos as well as with recent experiences of violence and disintegration, politics bears the responsibility of assuring that the community persists, that it survives beyond the futility of the singular life. We can observe the difficult balance between innovation and duration in the ambiguities of democracy. Contrasting with the tyrant's arbitrariness, democracy establishes laws that restrain citizens as well as public officials in the future. However, together with the rule of law, the principles of popular sovereignty and majority rule imply that nothing is irrevocable and that every decision may be revised. Hence the difficult management of time.

Second, the contingent nature of decision making puts the political task of formulating desired objectives under a heavy strain. As the 'art of the possible' politics is called upon to reconcile the desirable with the necessary. I would like to highlight the difficult elaboration of societal goals at this point. In reality agreements on objectives are as important as those on procedures in the game of democracy. Politics aims not just at constructing the future. It wants to construct it deliberately according to a certain project, an image of a desired future. Moreover, in essence all politics justifies itself by means of references to a better tomorrow. The 'aura' of politics lies in this promise. By delimiting the horizons of 'what is desired' and 'what is possible', democratic deliberation serves as the modern, cooperative and institutional method of managing societal uncertainty. Yet, though the most noble aspect of politics lies in the formulation of social objectives, its daily exercise is ruled by contingency and constraint, that is, by a limited 'menu' of uncertain options. In everyday politics, necessities (real or apparent) often leave little room for choices. The 'necessary' always presents itself with great urgency. There is no time left. And often this scarcity of time dramatically limits the range of available alternatives.

There are two phenomena which, in my opinion, clearly illustrate the current awareness of temporal factors: information technology and ecology. A widespread fascination exists for the world of computers and its steady stream of innovations. Underlying this fascination is an eagerness to gain time. Yet the acceleration of time turns things into fleeting events. The new discoveries – which are actually successive developments of the same product – fail to produce anything qualitatively new. It seems to be a hallmark of our epoch that its advances fail to generate new horizons. The prevailing slogan is 'more of the same'. This pattern of unlimited consumption contrasts, however, with the notorious interest in preserving the environment. Alongside the admiration for the quick and transient comes an increasing concern for conservation – but conservation in relation to nature. In other words the current desire for permanence is no longer based on a consciousness of history. Rather, time is taken as being natural and therefore, reified notions of natural time are crowding out older concepts of historical time.

Our consciousness of time no longer relies on tradition. Nor does it rely on the revolution of the *status quo*. Instead it withdraws into a permanent present which freezes history. The relationship between past, present and future, through which we try to understand social processes as historic processes, is weakened by the overpowering irruption of an omnipresent present. There seems to be no other time than the present. On the one hand the ghosts of the past are watching us. Despite all our efforts to create memory, history vanishes into thin air, only to survive in the form of mythical visions. Without a doubt the past continues to have its effects on the present, but it is no longer available as practical experience. On the other hand the future dissipates. It turns into a simple projection of the current state of affairs. Therefore the course of events loses relevance as well as depth. It becomes flat and shallow. When the future is reduced to electoral timetables, statistical projections or negotiation schedules the very notion of the future becomes insignificant.

The culture of images, which is so characteristic of our times, illustrates well how all that is solid melts into instants, substitutes and simulacra. When time is consumed in a voracious repetition of fleeting images – just like a video clip – reality evaporates and at the same time becomes overwhelming.

The acceleration of time prevents the political system from elaborating societal goals and thus from opening up common horizons, a shared future. Promises for a better future are reduced to improvements for certain sectors. They may provide important benefits to specific social groups but they lack any reference to joint projects. Even allusions to concepts of order that would transcend immediacy are missing. Politics consequently fails in its mission to construct shared frameworks of reference.

Under the impact of the market politics loses some of its vital dimensions. Instead of discovering and formulating the citizenry's self-determined goals, politics tends to confine itself to reacting to external challenges. The calculation of given opportunities becomes a substitute for reflecting on desired states of future. The public agenda therefore resembles an outdated inventory more than a guide for discussing alternatives for the future.

The retraction of the temporal dimension provokes a crisis of leadership. Politics confronts more and more difficulties in making sense of the future and conferring meaning to societal processes. To my understanding this contributes decisively to the loss of the interpretative codes mentioned above. To a large extent, political leadership consists precisely in offering mental maps that permit the citizenry to recognize itself as a community of citizens.

With the erosion of interpretative codes, the future ceases to be intelligible and predictable. And it is no longer subject to common action. Citizens experience the loss of political guidance as a loss of perspective. Their collective imaginations no longer manage to anticipate the course of events, and therefore all notions of order shrink to the here and now. Because of this lack of perspective, the situation seems out of control. And abandoned in a world without clear boundaries, people lose confidence in politics.

To the degree that its governing capacity is weakened, politics becomes more and more similar to business management. Of course improving public management is a prominent task in Latin America and we should therefore avoid confusing the two concepts. Management is based on instrumental rationality, on the choice of proper means for ends which are given, while defining those ends is the task of politics. However, as I have already pointed out, politics encounters manifest difficulties in discussing and selecting the objectives of social development in our times. In losing its reference to societal goals, political action is increasingly reduced to economic management. In our internationalized economies no policy can ignore such data as productivity, inflation, investment and exchange rates and so on. However managing macroeconomic constraints is not the same thing as elevating macroeconomic equilibria to guiding normative principles of political action.

Political society finds itself more and more constrained by the economy through 'technical imperatives'. It is definitely healthy that politics now respects the dynamics of other societal spheres and refrains from pretensions to control economic processes (remember, for example, recent experiences in Latin America and Eastern Europe). But in doing so, tasks which are specifically political are often relinquished. A kind of naive veneration of the market places an unduly high value on economic efficiency to the detriment of other vital dimensions of societal coexistence. This coexistence depends on 'hard' economic data as well as on 'soft' changeable constellations of symbols and collective imaginations. Politics degenerates into a self-referential activity when it fails to take these cultural aspects of a democratic 'community of citizens' into account.

REDRAWING OUR POLITICAL MAPS

Our incipient inquiries into the meaning of democracy and democratic politics lead us to a double phenomenon. We can observe a certain 'neutralization' of democratic politics as its capacity to order and direct social processes is questioned and even paralyzed. It would be erroneous, however, to blame democratic institutions or politicians for this regressive process. To my understanding, the problem lies in the cultural realm. Underneath the retreat of politics we find a loss of perspective, a loss of cognitive means to make the present intelligible and to guide the construction of a common future. And to the extent that politics loses its dynamic force, its image becomes blurred. The current disenchantment with the institutionalized forms of democratic politics is linked to the crisis of orientation and the loss of purpose that we have discussed. People no longer know what to think of politics. Today, politics tends to confine its responsibilities to such an extent that one is forced to ask startling questions about the residual meaning of democracy. This uncertainty affects our ways of conducting politics. If we do not know what to expect from democracy, we can easily develop distorted views of what is feasible in politics. This also has consequences for the way we evaluate democratic politics. If politics no longer sets the course for societal development, its value becomes ambivalent or undecidable.

In the current context of major transformations, politics is suffering from an apparent deficiency. If we want to adapt ourselves to the new situation, we have to redefine politics. We have to update the maps we formerly used to determine the importance and the meaning we ascribe to democratic politics. This is a practical exercise, not an academic one. And it is also a cultural exercise if we comprehend political culture as production and reproduction of 'the political'. I am referring especially to the interpretive codes through which we structure and orient political life. With the erosion of ideological and cognitive maps, the cleavages which have provided structure to the political world fade away. It would be shortsighted, however, to confuse the loss of political creativity we are experiencing, and which is reflected in the reigning mood of political malaise, with depoliticization. Quite the contrary, politics is facing a process of transformation.

As we have seen, recharting political maps implies the reformulation of spatial coordinates.[4] It also means redefining the scales we operate with. Currently the use of small-scale maps predominates. Such maps provide us with meticulous information. For instance they enable us to identify in detail the exact location actors occupy in the political space. However this type of map generates too much information. The informational excess it produces makes it difficult to discern which points are significant and thus creates obstacles to the design of medium- and long-term strategies. What we need are large-scale maps, which are more useful for approaching a globalized field, for reconstructing relationships between multiple levels, and thus for establishing workable criteria of orientation.

A second factor involved in processes of cartographic restructuring is symbolization. Maps operate as symbolic representations of reality. Through them we find out what is 'real' and what is 'possible'. They form a symbolic universe which has undergone a complete transformation. The weakening of the state, once in charge of representing society, reflects a generalized erosion of collective symbols. It is around these symbols that conflicts over the meaning of democratic politics focus. To the degree that the democratic order loses its symbolic density and consistency, the people's bonds to and their identification with democracy will weaken. Redrawing our political maps therefore presupposes the restoration of democracy's symbolic force as a collective enterprise.

All maps are based on a projection of space starting from a central axis. This structure inevitably highlights some points while marginalizing others. At present our standard map, which is based on the centrality of politics, is being put into question. Today the international bipolarity has collapsed, the national framework of politics is crumbling, and processes of globalization and fragmentation are reaching startling heights. This intersection of critical processes is destroying our former certainties regarding the proper place of politics. At this point we do not even know what the central political issues are. Political positions appear as 'collages' in which different and contradicting elements are juxtaposed in fluid kaleidoscopic configurations. Hence strategies of minimal consistency and durability no longer exist. We must therefore attempt to recompose political perspectives which restore our ability to establish priorities. This leads us to the temporal dimension and with it to the notion of the future.

As we have seen, the acceleration of time has undermined our images of the future. Without horizons we confound the existing with the necessary, and the generation of alternatives is blocked. To a large degree this explains the anachronistic impression democratic politics conveys. It appears outdated. Incapable of formulating objectives that would transcend immediacy and thus reduced to an uninspiring choice of lesser evils, politics is held hostage by contingency. However, while this 'omnipresent present' raises questions about the steering capacity of politics, it does not eradicate the concern for the future. The longing for a better tomorrow continues to exist. It may take regressive forms (as in different types of fundamentalism) and feed antipolitical movements which are incompatible with liberal democracy. But it may also advance the development of democracy. For that to happen, however, we need to rethink our notion of time and, in particular, our idea of the future.

One final observation: reconstructing cognitive maps means reconstructing the rationality currently in use. Since the Age of Enlightenment, modernity has striven to illuminate darkness with the radiance of reason. In reality, however, any theory or concept illuminates some aspects and leaves others in the dark. In our perplexity we may recur to a different, perhaps less 'illuminist' experience of everyday life. We may turn off the lights until our eyes become accustomed to the darkness and then spot the shadows. What I wish to say is: perhaps we should temporarily suspend our familiar conceptions in order to visualize the emergent contours of new democratic realities.

Notes

*   This chapter was translated by Andreas Schedler with the aid of Jane Schröder and Marcela Ríos. An initial draft was published in Spanish under the title 'Los nuevos perfiles de la política', *Nueva Sociedad*, vol. 130 (March–April 1994).

1.   C. Maier, 'Democracy and its Discontents', *Foreign Affairs*, vol. 73, no. 4 (July–August 1994).

2.   K. Polanyi, *La gran transformación* (Mexico: Fondo de Cultura Económica, 1992; originally published in 1944).

3.   See, for example, Banco Inter-Americano de Desarrollo, *Reforma social y pobreza* (Washington, DC: BID-UNDP, 1993).

4.   Credit for the mapping criteria must go to Santos Boaventura de Sousa, 'Una cartografía simbólica de las representaciones sociales', *Nueva Sociedad*, vol. 116 (November–December 1991).

Name Index

Subject Index